ALREADY GONE

ALREADY GONE

Forty Stories of Running Away

Edited by Hannah Grieco

Alan Squire Publishing
Bethesda, Maryland

Alan Squire Publishing

Already Gone: Forty Stories of Running Away is published by Alan Squire Publishing, Bethesda, MD.

© 2023 Alan Squire Publishing

Printed in the Unites States of America
ISBN (print): 978-1-942892-36-6
ISBN (epub): 978-1-942892-37-3

Library of Congress Control Number: 2023940280

Jacket design and cover art by Randy Stanard
Author photo by Gretchen Edwards
Copy editing and interior design by Nita Congress
Interior art: Real_life_photo/Shutterstock; Ekaterina Glazkova/
    Adobe Stock; pzAxe/Adobe Stock
Printing consultant: Steve Waxman
Printed by Carter Printing Company

First Edition
Ordo Vagorum

CONTENTS

I

How to Fly Away 3
   Caroljean Gavin

Mother's Day.. 5
   Deesha Philyaw

A Girl Attends a Pep Rally 17
   Ruth Joffre

In the Wings, No One Can Hear You Scream 21
   Lori Yeghiayan Friedman

More Fun in the New World 25
   Amy Stuber

That Kind of Love 35
   Melissa Llanes Brownlee

How to Reverse Time When You're Tired of Being the
   Hero 37
   Amber Sparks

Hive Mind... 45
   Melissa Bowers

Surface Treatments 49
   Zach Powers

Held Under 53
   Kathleen McKitty Harris

A Good Run of It 59
  Edie Meade

In the Company of Sadie Star. 63
  Jamy Bond

Suddenly, a Man. 67
  Hananah Zaheer

Transformista. 73
  aureleo sans

Times He Touched Her in the Night 79
  Aubrey Hirsch

Quiet Hours 83
  Lilly Dancyger

II

The Chase. 91
  K.C. Mead-Brewer

Circling Back 93
  Matt Cantor

Self-Care 103
  Sarah Tollok

Sandwiched 107
  DW McKinney

Corpse Mom Discovers the Ten-Step Korean Skin Care
  Routine. 113
  Hema Nataraju

To the Man at the Pump Next to Me at the BP in Marble
  Hill on the Night of My Husband's Birthday after I've
  Kicked My Family Out of an Almost Moving Car . . . 117
  Emily James

Solve for Ways to Disappear. 121
  Alysia Li Ying Sawchyn

It's Exactly What You Think...................... 125
  Matthew E. Henry

The Girl with a Painted Tongue.................... 129
  Tara Isabel Zambrano

Leave Me in the Sun 133
  Michael B. Tager

III

Lines of Communication.......................... 149
  Miriam Gershow

Before the Big Bang.............................. 157
  Kelsey Francis

Blueprint for an Elopement........................ 161
  Megha Nayar

Typical Calls of the Red-Tailed Hawk............... 169
  Kate Gehan

Tammy's Tamagotchi 171
  Davon Loeb

Inheritance...................................... 173
  Ellen Birkett Morris

Feeding Time 183
  Jen Soong

Escape.. 187
  DeMisty D. Bellinger

Underwater Even Bells Sound Like Bodies 191
  Chloe N. Clark

Fenix Pepper.................................... 195
  Matt Barrett

The Easter Bunny and the Theoretical Mass 199
  Caroline Macon Fleischer

Pocketed 209
    Sarah Fawn Montgomery

When They Come for the Wolves. 213
    Anna Gates Ha

Hummingbirds in the Forest of Needle and Blood. 217
    Ahimsa Timoteo Bodhrán

INTRODUCTION

You wanna fly, you got to give up the shit that weighs you down. —*Toni Morrison,* Song of Solomon

There's something unexpected and magical about editing an anthology. The gathering of written work from a variety of writers, pieced together into something bigger, something more. We could search for the perfect metaphor, perhaps different shades of paint that add to the texture and nuance of a portrait. Or we could liken it to the planting of seeds in a garden that will eventually yield an entire summer's worth of fruit. Editing an anthology is a tremendous effort, just like painting or gardening, and it also involves a similar moment of transformation. The instant those layers of color reveal cheekbones and a nose on the canvas. A face appears out of murky swirls. Or the first strawberry, red on the vine, an explosion of flavor born in an empty plot.

As you read and edit and sort and imagine—all of a sudden it hits you, what you're witnessing. Story after exceptional story begin to fuse together into something entirely new. Magic.

For this anthology, I asked writers to send us their prose about running away. And the stories they sent! Mothers flew, literally and figuratively, from their families. Wives sped down highways. Children turned into wild beasts and fled their homes. A man spent his life savings first on the stars, and then on a spaceship to reach them. Narratives of secret marriages, of loss, of death, of the afterlife as an escape. An essay about the city streets at night. Stories about college and freedom, about setting down the mantle of hero, about painting, even—layer upon layer, but this time to create a barrier, to escape by constructing new walls.

Maybe we all want to run away. Maybe there's a voice inside each of us that resists being rooted, that speaks to generations past when we wandered for food and chased the sun to stay warm. Or maybe this world is simply too heavy these days, weighing us down, flattening us until we finally say, "No more." And if we can't release the burden in real life, perhaps the page is where we turn. To examine what we hold, to imagine what it means to let go. If we fly on the page, maybe we can fly off the page, as well.

There is always escape in reading. But here, we'll go much, much further. Here, we'll break the rules and spit in the eye of convention. Here we'll fill the tank, hit the gas, and fly.

Thank you for coming with us. We're so glad you're along for the ride.

Hannah Grieco
June 2, 2023

HOW TO FLY AWAY

Caroljean Gavin

Wake up just before dawn. Check your phone the night before to see what time the sun is scheduled to rise. Don't set your alarm. You don't want your husband to wake up at the chimes. Think to yourself "Wake up at five, wake up at five, wake up at five..." until you fall asleep and wake up at five, amazed but not surprised. Roll out of bed carefully. Do not bother with extra clothes or foot coverings. You won't need them. Soon. You know you won't need them soon.

Leave out the front door, silently, locking it behind you. Wade out through the flowers, through the wet grass that's been moaning for a mowing. Close your eyes. Feel the end of night on your face. Hear the trees flapping their hands in the breeze. See the lightening. Behind your eyes. Keep your eyes closed. You are in the midst of a waking-up song. The chitters, cheeps, peeps, trills. Taste the opening of your throat. Do not open your mouth. Keep the song. You don't want the neighborhood to hear what you're becoming, and besides, you don't know the language yet. You don't know your own language yet.

Your body is changing. Each feather takes root in your skin and sprouts into a spreading softness. Your bones, too, are hollowing out. You have never felt this delicate. You steady your talons in the ground, and you take a little hop. The hop pulls you up, up. Why would you try to stop something that feels so good, that feels so right? Your eyes open, they do not break, or pop, or burst open. They simply open and rejoice.

You wheel around your house for a while. You hear your son rising, singing songs to himself, tossing cars around his room. You make several passes across his window. He is safe. Nothing will harm him in there. Your husband is still sleeping, he will wake up soon enough.

And when your husband wakes up, he will be confused you aren't there, he will call your phone, he will hear your phone buzzing on the nightstand, he will figure you just went out for a run, he will take care of your son, he will start to get worried as the day goes on. He will call your friends, your family.

You will be back. You are not leaving them forever. You will be back in time for dinner. You will weigh down your body with cutlery, and you will pull the feathers out of your skin. You will pick them up something for dinner. You will come up with a reason that is a surprise.

You would never, never, ever leave your family forever, only life happened so fast, and you never got to soar over the ocean. Never got a chance to dip a wing as a whale spouted. Never got to perch on the mast of a boat. You never had the chance to feel clouds disappear into your eyes. You never had the chance to see the horizon in all directions. You push yourself up higher, higher, higher, and this time you choose your wind.

MOTHER'S DAY

DEESHA PHILYAW

left as my kids slept, but I stuck a note on the refrigerator because I didn't want them to think I left like their daddy left when Josiah, my youngest, was still in diapers, without no explanation, only to be heard from again when he felt like it, which was about every other year. Just up and left and started another family cross town, a wife and two kids.

Every December since Josiah was born, I told myself that that winter would be my last in the ashy town I was born and raised in and where I raised my kids. It's gray there even in spring. I kept saying I'm-a move someplace with colors all year round. Yellow, orange, and red fall leaves, bright yellow tulips, grass so green it looks fake, and a clean blue ocean that I can drive to in a heartbeat. A place with all the colors, like the boxes of sixty-four Crayolas my mama used to get us for Christmas. The kind with the sharpener built into the box. I don't think I ever sharpened a crayon once, but I liked knowing I could, if I wanted to. That's how I felt about living in my hometown. I'm not the type to rip and run in the streets all the time the way my best friend Misty does. But when I do choose to be out and about, I want sunshine on my face and on my scalp and on my bare shoulders and in between my toes. And more than that, I don't want to have to take care of anybody other than my damn self. Not even house plants.

It took me a week to write that goodbye note to my kids. What to say? I couldn't tell them that I'd left to chase colors and sunshine and freedom. That I was sick of the familiar. That their father isn't the only one who gets to start over. That I love them, but don't want to be around them all the time. How do you tell your kids that for you, active motherhood was a season? That you're ready to...move on? Sounds like a breakup. Can you break up with your kids? Can you "it's not you, it's me" your kids? Do you tell them how you'd never had a chance to figure out who you are, other than somebody's mama, somebody's daughter, and somebody's discarded wife? How you never had a chance, until now?

I don't expect my kids to understand and be happy for me. They have every right to be upset with me. And I had every right to leave.

For eighteen years, I dreamed about leaving. As I rocked and nursed Josiah to sleep, I would hum goodbye songs. "Midnight Train to Georgia," "Hit the Road Jack," "Urge for Going" (Misty laughed at me, but I like that white lady, Joni Mitchell. Her songs anyway.) Hearing all those gotta-go tunes is probably why Josiah is such a restless chap, as my mama used to call him when he got to running all over her house and standing up, bouncing at the dinner table like he had ants in his pants. The worst punishment I could give him was to make him stay in the house, even though there really wasn't much to do in that town no way. Misty say she gon' die there. Why would you even be thinking about that in your forties? She say other places are nice—she ain't been nowhere but Disney World, Atlanta, New York City, and on the

Caribbean cruise ships—but home is home, and that's where she's going to breathe her last.

Not me. I left that bitch. (The town, not Misty.) And I didn't take my kids with me. But they grown.

*

In Miami I have a job, even though I don't need one. Part time at a liquor store walking distance from my house. I got the job on a lark, a few months after I got here. I was in the store to pick up my usual order— Tanqueray, Patron, Moscato, Riunite Lambrusco Red, Asti Spumante, and some wine coolers. I could have my order delivered, but I try to walk everywhere as much as possible. I ain't never been into gyms, but I am trying to live at least forty-two more years. Anyway, that particular day, my usual guy wasn't there and the new guy couldn't find my order behind the counter where it was supposed to be. So I'm reading my list off to the new guy, this bald guy with a nice lil goatee, and he says to me, "Baby, slow down."

Now, I always been a fast talker. Folks back home was just used to it, I guess.

Also, I couldn't remember the last time somebody called me "baby."

I eyed New Guy up and down, took a deep breath, and started over, slow and kinda sexy-like.

New Guy looked me up and down and didn't bother to hide the fact that he liked what he saw. In Miami, I'm back out, toes out, seven days a week, including sport sandals for my early evening strolls on the beach. Sport sandals ain't nobody's idea of cute, but I keep a fresh pedicure. Always a minty green or a Tiffany blue or pale pink. That day in the liquor store, I wore a backless sundress with a floral and strawberry print and some sparkly flip-flops.

I said to New Guy, "Does your manager know you check out the lady customers like this?" But I said it with a smile.

"He does," New Guy said, extending his hand. "I'm Rick. The manager."

And that's how I met Rick. I work at the store on Tuesdays and Thursdays, and he stays over at my place a few nights a week. We don't make it no more complicated than that.

*

I had to leave my mama's house when I turned eighteen. It wasn't nothing personal; me and both my siblings had to go after high school. Mama said, "Military, college, or a job." Those were your options, but you had to make your own way. I didn't have the grades for a scholarship like my sister Katina, or the physical fitness for the military like my brother Kev. So I went to work. Or rather I kept working. I been working since I was fourteen years old, as soon as I was old enough to get a work permit. I went to get it on my fourteenth birthday. That's how bad I wanted to work and make my own money and be less of a burden on my mama who was raising us by herself without any help.

By the time I left home, I was working two jobs and pregnant with my first child, my son Jamari.

I always wanted to make things easier for my kids. In my house, turning eighteen didn't come with an eviction notice.

I left my mama's house after graduation and moved right into another woman's house, my mother-in-law's.

Her son was one of those no-count private school boys whose father drank and whose mother was a good Christian lady who made a career outta keeping up appearances. She called me a fool when I wouldn't take the money for an abortion. But she bought me a dress and she smiled real big in the photos of our shotgun wedding officiated by her pastor in the backyard of their McMansion. Later, she called me *country* for sleeping with my babies and breastfeeding them. I knew she was the kind of woman who never got drunk off the smell of her baby's milk breath or delighted in his chubby hands exploring her face in the quiet hours before daybreak. And I pitied her.

*

Have you lost your goddamn mind?

Misty called and left a voicemail. I listened to it as I stepped out of first class and walked to baggage claim at MIA. I listened to it before reading the dozens of text messages from my kids, imagining a time when Misty would be done cussing me out and might come to visit. I listened to her message on repeat riding in the Lyft to the title company to close on my new house. I purchased it based on photos online, with the help of my attorney.

For real Jalisa. What the fuck? Where are you? Call me!

I texted Misty instead. *I'm fine, M. I promise.*

I also replied to my kids on the way to the title company. Each one had texted me—texted, not called, mind you—thinking I'd left because of something they had done. Or not done. I responded to them in birth order:

No, Jamari, I'm not mad that you brought my car back on E again. Matter fact, that's your car now. I'm signing the title over to you.

Yes, Jeraden, I was sick and tired of you keeping dishes full of rotting food in your bedroom. But that ain't why I left.

Jenaya, you're right. I don't appreciate you having Damon in my house after I told you his thieving ass was not welcome. I know you can do much, much better, daughter mine. But you have to believe that.

Josiah, I know you're sorry you failed the drug test for the internship I got set up for you. Like I tried to tell you, weed is not your friend when you're working for someone else. I forgive you, but you've got to forgive yourself, baby.

I almost got back on a plane and went back. Almost.

*

These days, kids don't run away from home anymore, unless they are really troubled. Every third show on TV is some detective drama or true-crime program reminding them how crazy people are out in the streets. Plus, kids got it too good now, too comfortable at home, to leave. So they stay their soft asses put.

One time, in 1987, I had the nerve to fix my eight-year-old mouth to tell my mama I was running away. I don't even remember what set me off. Probably Mama saying no to something I really wanted to do. She ran a tight ship and "no" was her favorite word. I just remember running into the bathroom and slamming the door like a white girl on a TV sitcom. Cardinal rules in Janice Bailey's house: Don't be leaving her front door open letting out all the air in the summertime. Cut off the lights when you leave a room. *Don't* slam her doors.

Well, I slammed a door. And then the house went dead quiet.

I sat on the side of the tub until Kev came home from football practice funky and in need of a shower. He threatened to kick the door in if I didn't open it.

I tried to sprint from the bathroom into the bedroom I shared with Katina, but Mama caught me by my arm and pulled me onto the front porch where a small suitcase filled with my clothes was waiting for me. She didn't say a word. Just left me on the porch all night with the suitcase. I never threatened to run away again.

*

I left at daybreak on Mother's Day, in honor of my mama who died in her empty nest having never flown very far to see more of the world. I wondered why she never flew away and stayed gone. She had the freedom to do it, no kids tying her down. Mama would never admit it, but I suspect she was afraid to fly (on a plane), never learned to drive, and wanted no parts of anything she couldn't control. She didn't even like to eat out because hardly anyone else's cooking was up to her standards. Mama liked things familiar.

*

Am I a good mother? Have I been the mother each of my kids needed me to be? I've wrestled with these questions since Josiah was born, and I've decided that I have been a good enough mother. Certainly not the best. But good enough. I tried. I really did.

My middle babies, Jeraden and Jenaya, weren't planned, but they weren't oops babies either. I loved being a mother. My ex was actually a decent human being at the time, and it felt like we were playing house. We both worked, but his parents still let us live with

them rent free and they paid our daycare bill. They
made it too easy not to think about birth control. And
I didn't pay my mother-in-law no mind, with her slick
comments about me being a baby factory.

When Jeraden was almost eighteen months, I found
out I was pregnant with Jenaya. We needed more space.
My in-laws gave us the down payment for a house, the
one I just left. Then Jenaya was born, and she was
Daddy's Little Girl. Until Daddy started coming home
later and later, and staying gone longer and longer, until
he wasn't there no more. On one rare night that he was
home, before he left for good, we made Josiah.

My ex worked for his daddy and got paid mostly
under the table, so his income on paper—and the child
support—could be whatever he wanted it to be.

So even with child support, I had to take a second,
part-time job. Most nights, I was so tired, I didn't even
make it upstairs to my bed. Just fell asleep right in the
recliner in the living room. In the morning, I'd wake up
with a blanket over me. I will say this about my kids:
They're sweet, deep down. Every one of them, even the
ones who no longer speak to me.

                                    *

Don't you miss us?

Josiah texted that to me late one night. I had been
gone about a week. I didn't see the message until the
next morning because most nights, I'm sleep by ten.

I miss the jokes that no one is in on but the five of
us. The little sayings we've made up over the years.
Our family language. I miss Josiah still laughing all
high-pitched the same way he did when he was ten. I
miss Jamari laying his big ol' twenty-four-year-old head

in my lap for me to massage his scalp. I miss Jenaya singing off-key for her life to Whitney Houston. We all love Whitney Houston. And I miss Jeraden calling me "Mamacita." I don't remember when or why he started doing that. But I love it.

What I don't miss is their assumption that someone will take care of the things they can't be bothered with, that someone will always pick up the pieces, clean up their messes, ride their emotional roller coasters, come up with a Plan B after they fuck up a perfectly good Plan A. And that I'm that someone.

Maybe that's why Mama kicked Katina, Kev, and me out. Not so we could fly, but so we couldn't take her for granted anymore.

Yes, I texted Josiah back. *I miss y'all.*

*

It's December now. Back home, there's a winter storm. I'm sitting outside in the Miami sun eating Bahamian food for lunch. Just got off the phone with Misty. She started speaking to me again about a month after I left. She's coming to visit. We gonna ring in the new year together. I might even let Rick meet her.

I call my kids once a month. I call, it's up to them to answer. Jeraden won't speak to me, and he won't accept the monthly allowance I offer. Me and Jeraden have always run hot and cold. I don't know what it is. Mothers say they love their kids all the same. But how can we? The kids ain't the same, and who we are with them ain't the same.

Jamari doesn't answer my calls either, but he accepts the monthly allowance, and he stays in our old house, which I deeded over to Josiah.

Jenaya has a house of her own. I'll be damned if I let her become her brothers' maid. Her allowance covers the mortgage, her tuition, and other expenses so she never has to put up with some man's bullshit to survive. We talk, but I can tell she's hurt.

I'm still their mother, just from afar.

*

The first time Josiah came to visit me, he was surprised at my lil bungalow. Said he thought I'd buy a bigger house. I said for what? Bigger means more to take care of, which means more money to spend taking care of it. I'm planning on living a long time, and I need this money to last.

And he asked if he could stay. Move here and stay with me.

"No," I told him. "Go. Anywhere. Everywhere. You never liked to sit still. Don't start now."

Since then, Josiah's done some traveling and started his own landscaping and snow removal company. Now he's twenty-one-years old, managing a team of a dozen employees. That old gray town keeps my son in business.

During that last winter I lived at home, a few days after Josiah's eighteenth birthday, I claimed my winnings, the largest in the state's history. And for five months, I didn't say a word to anyone.

*

May 8, 2022

My dear babies:

By the time you read this, I'll be headed to my new home. I won the lottery, and I am tired. There are meals in the deep freezer and money in the envelopes with your names on them on the kitchen table. I will send more, and I will call you soon. If there's an emergency, call Misty. Or 911.

Love forever,

Mama

*

Jeraden called last night. He wants to come see me. I tell him anytime is good except January and February. I don't tell him that's when I'm going to Africa to see some other colors. First stop: Senegal. They have a pink lake there.

A GIRL ATTENDS A PEP RALLY

Ruth Joffre

On the walk home from the bus, she practices what she will say about her day. *There was a pep rally this afternoon. Principal ~~Wheezely~~ Weasley gave a speech ~~I didn't bother listening to~~, then the cheerleaders made a pyramid. ~~Gina winked at me from the top. Her cheeks were painted with school colors, and her hair was tied back with a red ribbon I gave her for her half-birthday. It was part of a set of primary and secondary colors, purchased not because they reminded me of rainbows but because I know she wants to be a graphic designer one day. She practices her skills by Photoshopping me into photos her family takes of her on vacation. Here we are walking Ruby, the Irish setter. Here we are collecting broken shells on a cold, rocky beach. Here we are posing in front of a waterfall just moments after I kissed her on the cheek. Her family is okay with it; her family knows. When I go to her house, her mother makes champurrado and rice pudding. We eat at the dining room table and aren't forced to say grace. We're not forced to say anything.~~*

As soon as she walks in, the interrogation begins.

What classes did you have today? *English, physics, history.*

Don't you have four classes a day? *French was canceled for the pep rally.*

A likely story, he says. What was the pep rally for? *The football game tonight.*

Who are they playing? *I'm not sure. I don't think it's as important as my studies.*

That's true. You don't have the physique for an athletic scholarship anyway, he says. Did you have any tests today? *One, on ~~U.S. imperialism and interference in Latin America~~ the rise of communism in Cuba, Nicaragua, and other Latin American nations.*

When will you get the results? *A few days.*

Bring me the exam when you get it back. I want to see the questions. *Okay.*

How much homework do you have? *A fair amount.*

Better get to work then. *Yes.*

This is the calmest part of her day. She stretches out on the floor of her bedroom, lays out her notebooks and textbooks, and disappears into other people's problems. If Jennifer is traveling at 60 mph on a level surface, assuming a coefficient of static friction of 0.75 and kinetic friction of 0.67, precisely how fucked is she if she hits that wall? If Cyrano de Bergerac were alive today and desperately in love, how easily could he trick his beloved with a deepfake? Does the existence of a Cher Guavara shirt imply the existence of a Chair Guavara shirt? In 5,000 words, prove that the rise of capitalism has resulted in the proliferation of modern slave labor and doomed the planet in its never-ending quest for capital. Now argue the exact opposite—jk, there aren't two sides to this argument. Your father is wrong. He is always wrong.

He is a lawyer. His home office is directly below her bedroom. On calls, his voice booms, the sound rising through the slats in the floorboards. He doesn't like her to listen to his calls. One time, she asked about an unfamiliar legal term she overheard ("arrears"), and he snapped, "Never you mind. Don't meddle in my affairs." Now whenever he's on a call she puts on music, wearing only one earbud in case he calls her name suddenly. He expects immediate responses, acceptable answers. He does not allow her to talk to her friends. Whenever she needs to make a call, he dials the number for her in order to match whoever picks up to the name she gives: *Gina Marcano. We have calculus together. I want to ask her a question about this problem.*

After handing her the receiver, he crosses his arms, monitoring her behavior.

What she says is, "Hey. I'm confused about problem two. How do you solve for 'e'?" but what she means is, *I love you. He's standing right here,* and because they have rehearsed this and because Gina's soft phone voice doesn't carry, she ignores the calculus question; they both know there's no solving for *e,* anyway. Her real reason for calling is to fantasize about the future. In six months, both girls will leave Vancouver, Washington, to attend Carnegie Mellon University, where Gina will study electronic and time-based media in the School of Art and where her father, the lawyer, thinks she'll be pre-law, though she really plans to study comparative literature and move in with Gina, who has found afford-able off-campus housing.

"We can get a one-bedroom. I'll grow sage, rosemary. You can finally get a smartphone."

Deep in the back of her mind, the image forms: of a normal day (brisk, partly sunny) with no interrogations, no rehearsed calls, no random room searches, only life, all those little moments of life she has only read about in books, like sleeping in, making love in the morning light, eating cereal out of a coffee mug because you're late and in a hurry, rushing between classes, pausing at lunch to say hello, goodbye, see you later, and the very concept of later, the thought of being out, not locked in her bedroom, at three, at four, after dinner, when the world, she has heard, twinkles with neon and puddles are shimmering reflections of everything she loves: Gina and ramen and a breed of spaniel she calls Sweet Prince instead of Cavalier King Charles because the rank suits it better. While her heart swells at this idea of the future, her face remains attentive, even confused. She pretends to look down at the differential equation and have a revelation. "I didn't realize that was possible. Thank you."

IN THE WINGS, NO ONE CAN HEAR YOU SCREAM

Lori Yeghiayan Friedman

The Most Loved Actress and the Least Loved Actress are waiting in the wings for the house lights to go down and the music to start, their cue to enter. Swaths of velvety cloth hang from the ceiling surrounding them like a chrysalis, the only thing separating them from the audience, and their cacophonous symphony of voices, mere feet away in the black box theater. No one can see them. No one even knows they are there.

Among the audience are their teachers and fellow classmates at the Prestigious Acting School where they are in the third and final year of an MFA program. *It sounds like a good time*, thinks Least, *being the ones about to sit in the dark*.

Tonight the chairs are arranged in rows, raked, theater-in-the-round-style with the "stage" in the middle, the performers in a pit which Least finds vaguely threatening, perhaps a vestige of its origins in Greco-Roman gladiator days, as if the crowd might at any moment morph into an uncontrolled mass, their individual desires concealed enough that they'd think nothing of throwing hunks of raw meat into the arena to whet the lion's appetite, cheering while it tore into them, shredding their flesh with its teeth and claws.

It's been a long three years at the Prestigious Acting
School. Least has been in a lot of plays with Most. Most
is petite, waiflike, sweet and whimsical, with blonde
hair and big, expressive blue eyes. Least is a brunette
with wide hips and a serious face. Tonight, Most is
playing a young girl who is going blind. Least is her
smothering mother.

The rehearsal process has been rough, at least for
Least. The Unpopular Director, a brittle woman in her
thirties with a severe red bob, has spent most of their
rehearsals shaking her head at Least, the sharp edge of
her hair slicing her pointed chin, saying:

"Can you try something different here? Just make
some choice different from the one you're making now."

"Most, you just keep doing what you're doing,"
Unpopular Director would say with an attempt at a
fanciful gesture, her hand flapping in the air.

The idea of choices had made Least think of Marjorie,
an actor she had known during her undergraduate
years. Marjorie was alabaster-skinned, auburn-haired
and super-talented, a few years older than the rest of
the students. Least wanted to be just like her: confident,
open, grounded, real onstage and in life. She ran into
her recently and was devastated to learn that Marjorie
was no longer acting, had become a teacher. "I love
teaching my students to make strong choices in their
work," Marjorie had said with her signature warmth,
"because life is about making choices."

Least has been playing mothers since the fourth
grade. She has always had the rounded limbs of a
mother; and, later, the ample bosom to match. Truth
be told, Least isn't all that nurturing. Most isn't all that
sweet, but her right-sized tits are. They are capped by

perfectly perky pink nipples that tilt up toward the lighting grid like baby bird beaks squawking *Feed me!*

Everyone is familiar with Most's tits, having seen them night after night during last spring's mainstage production: a revival of a 1920s German play about depressed medical students. At the climax of the play, Most rips off her blouse in an act of defiance, or something. Least played Most's most bitter rival in an ill-fitting wool suit and hideous red wig. During every performance, the Handsomest Actor who played Most's love interest would sneak over to where Least was waiting behind the set to make her entrance, post-tits-reveal moment, to get an eyeful, throwing Least a look that said: *Can you blame me?* And, frankly, she could not.

Least had invited Most to the beach one day during their first year. As they walked along the shore, the cold ocean stinging their bare feet, Least tried to spark a conversation. Most just smiled, revealing little. At rehearsal later that night, their classmate, Sad Clown Boy, had said:

"So, I heard you and Most went to the beach today and you spent the whole time apologizing for the weather."

Most and Least hadn't spent much time together alone since then until now.

"Sometimes just before I go onstage," whispers Most, out of their shared silence in the wings, "I think about running away." *Who would run away from being Most?*

"I mean, what would happen," continues Most, glancing over her shoulder and then looking directly into Least's eyes, "if we just walked out the door and never returned?"

Least, while unloved, has a reputation for being very responsible. Not showing up is not something she has considered. First, she imagines, the walls would break—the first, the second, the third, and the fourth!—and crumble into dust piles, releasing the velvet curtains which would land in a heap, before swirling back to life to go chasing Most and Least into the night. As Most and Least ran, the curtains would wrap around their torsos, the ends unfurling majestically behind them until they started to flap and ripple, like the pinions of a dragon, providing just the momentum they would need to lift them into the air toward the wide open sky. The audience, having raced out of their seats, would run after them, sensing the momentousness of the occasion—*What stagecraft! What will happen next!?*—spotting them in their altered forms, their dark wings streaking across the black sky. Most and Least would look back to see the crowd, note the red dot of Unpopular Director's hair, the astonished look on her face, though soon the crowd would no longer look like humans but stained cells clumped together against a background and then a landscape within a grid within a landmass, receding, then disappearing, eclipsed by the sheer size of the space into which Most and Least would be ascending as they transformed into creatures made of stardust burning bright, the beginning of all things, with the power to give birth to worlds.

As the house lights go down, Most and Least hear the first few notes of music. They step out onto the stage. Find their spots. Take their places. Wait in the dark for the light. Choose.

MORE FUN IN THE NEW WORLD

Amy Stuber

My mother is only fifty when my father dies of suicide in a mental health facility devoted solely to preventing such an outcome. Belts had been confiscated at check-in. His portable radio was taken apart with a screwdriver by a delicate-handed orderly searching its innards for blades and pills. One of a troupe of nurses tipped a head in his room every ten minutes. Suicide watch it was called, a spectator sport. Somehow, they'd missed a wire coat hanger bent over on itself time and again in the secret lining of his vintage suitcase, a case his own father had taken on a ship across the Atlantic in 1910, a secret lining into which his father had hidden Hungarian coins, a pocket watch, and a photo of his own mother.

People arrive with food after the funeral. Most of the food is ugly in rectangular vats and designed for quick consumption or freezing, as if we are feed cattle, which would have disgusted my father who'd organized orange slices in pretty fans on the plates of my childhood. My mother sits far back on the green velvet couch wearing a necklace my father bought for her when they first met. Its beads are the size of animal eggs, and it looks like the solar system if a giant strung it on wire to carry around with him. "We found it at an art fair in a little town north of San Francisco," I hear her saying over and over to this person and then that person. Her hands hold onto the beads—or are they stones?—like she's in water and they float and she—she knows it—absolutely does not.

I have two jobs that summer in between my first and second years of college (restaurant and retail). I stop showing up to both. There is then a series of days, maybe weeks, when I lie with my mother in the backyard on a down blanket, both of us face down and in defiance of the mosquitoes that machete our legs with blood and bites. I don't think we eat, but probably we do. Actually, yes, we eat. And by the end of this series of days or weeks, the lawn around the blanket is covered with food waste: fruit rinds, cellophane in colors, an overturned and empty container of rainbow sherbet. I'm not sure if it's weekday or weekend when we both leave in the car without plan or destination. I'm not even sure we close or lock the doors. "Take it all," my mother says from the driver's seat, making a sweeping motion with one hand. It's July, and all of the sprinklers up and down the block are ticking in the early morning in a way that sounds orchestral. The house is near the city's art gallery where people are lining up for family photos on the grounds of the sculpture garden. "Art! Seriously? Art?" my mother scoffs as we head west and out of the Midwestern city of my childhood.

We drive until we can't drive anymore and there are several things I could say about it:

1. The highway from Kansas City is one long left turn past old churches in farm fields and cows that couldn't give a shit and sometimes stand shoulder

high and side by side in oval ponds and birds that dip down and almost touch the windshield at sixty-five miles per hour but then manage to dart away at just the right moment.

2. You can listen to David Bowie's "Five Years" on cassette over and over (stop, rewind, stop, play, stop, rewind, repeat), that part where things go from measured to operatic more times than you might think, and it doesn't get old.

3. It's probably best not to stand arm in arm with your mother under an irrigation sprinkler on someone else's property, but the relentlessness of water can make you feel like you've peeled your skin back in a way that is both painful and necessary.

4. Much of the road from Durango, Colorado, to Farmington, New Mexico, is unsimple with switchbacks. You read true crime books aloud to your mother while she takes a turn too quickly, and yells, "Sheer drop-off to the right," and starts laughing hysterically. Another turn and then, "Sheer drop-off to the left!" She thinks it's funny, and though you do not, you give it to her. In the book you read aloud, Diane Downs, Oregon mother of three, has just pulled her car outside the entrance to her small town's emergency room and won't stop with the horn. All three of her children have been shot, and it's clear though not stated yet that she is the one to have shot them. "See?" your mother says as she winds around another turn and the tops of pine cut into clouds. "See? Things could be worse." But then she is crying and so are you.

5. It will become clear in some motel in Grand Junction or Wendover that your packing was haphazard. Your mother's opened suitcase holds linen pants and a few of your father's commemorative 10K T-shirts. You will have two rain jackets and no socks.

6. Do not let yourself realize that the series of postcards your father sent you from his last inpatient facility have been left behind in some truck stop bathroom in Abilene or Limon or Idaho Springs, those cards each penned with just one sentence: "I'm friends with a morbidly obese man named Aaron who knits" and "I'm beginning to like the forced tai chi" and "All the food here seems to be cantaloupe" and "None of this is your fault."

We end up in Las Vegas. This is before the food revolution, when there are mainly buffets and no famous chefs, and the hotel's entrance is a weird, sculptural lion so that we walk into the lion's neck if lions were giant and tan and stucco. "Who thought of this? Really, who?" my mother asks in a voice too loud, but it's Vegas so it doesn't matter. I can remember my father shh-ing her in several hotel lobbies on childhood vacations, but I also remember them standing close and forgetting I was in the room more than once. My mother is in a red "Hospital Hill 10K" T-shirt and wide-legged white linen pants. I'm in one of the raincoats snapped closed over a yellow bra, and it's 109 degrees outside but crisp inside with what I imagine is a building-sized air conditioner blasting the whole place, and it's all dizzy-making lights and smoke and women in sequined bikinis with trays of drinks adorning each palm. This, this living beyond a parent who has chosen not to, is a lot like walking after someone has cut off your feet.

First thing, we buy shirts and shorts and swimsuits in one of many gift shops and go—terry cloth and neon—to the pool, which is on the twenty-fifth floor, and where most of the people sitting in lounge chairs around the water are the old and the drinking. I jump in immediately and lie on the blue-painted bottom of the pool until I feel like my lungs will explode or implode, whatever lungs do when deprived of air for too long. When I come up, an older man with the kind of thick and perfect white hair of the patriarch in a soap opera is sitting in the chair next to my mother, and next to him is a boy who is maybe a little younger than I am but probably my age. His hair is over his eyes, he wears mailman shorts and old Vans, and he's reading *The Mysteries of Pittsburgh* like everyone else ages eighteen to twenty-two that summer.

"Hey," he says, and I say hey back, and then he goes back to his book and I spread out on the chair and cover my face with a towel and for many minutes listen to my mother talk to the man while she pretends to be someone else. She's from New York, she tells him. In truth, she was born in Pittsburgh and has lived most of her life in Kansas City. She's driving me to Stanford, she tells him. The reality is that I go to an unimpressive state school near the house where I grew up. Big family, yes, she tells him. She has no siblings. Owned a restaurant in Soho before selling it recently, she tells him. She can barely cook. My father made multicourse meals, while she smoked on the brick patio or played solitaire while listening to NPR at the kitchen table.

Finally, I fall asleep under the white tent of the towel and have the same dream about my father that I've been having every time I've fallen asleep since he died. I hate dreams, and I'd rather not have them, ever, because of the trick and mindfuck of them, because of the there and not there of them. But in this dream, my father is in a massive body of water. I'm on the shore, and my father is trying to save his sister, the aunt I never knew, the teenager my father and his brother were unable to rescue from drowning on a hot day in Joplin, Missouri, in 1955, the brother who went on to overdose intentionally in a hotel room in New Orleans. It was a family striated with tragedy and grief, and in the dream my mother is always this giant floating face behind my shoulder saying, "Of course," and then, "We all knew it was coming," and she's looking at my father as he is putting his own head under, and again she says, "We all knew," and really in real life, we all did.

When I wake up it's a higher level of drinking and drunkenness at the hotel pool, and my mother and the man are gone. The boy is asleep in the chair next to me with *The Mysteries of Pittsburgh* on his stomach rising and falling with his breath. The sky is still bright, but the outdoor lights have come on, and it's all hot and disorienting.

I elbow the boy and look over at the empty chairs. "Oh, hey," he says. He shakes his bangs to the side in a way I can tell he knows looks good. His legs have burned, and his shin bones look pink and shiny. I notice he has a ribbon of scars all the way up one leg, and I wonder: plate glass window, car accident, weird unshakable childhood infection?

"I think your mom went to the party with my grand-father. She told me to tell you," he says, and I try to do the weird age math that makes my mother and his grandfather a possible pairing but then give up. I don't let myself wonder where any of this is going: my mom and this grandfather, the hotel party. I don't want to know. Instead, I force myself to run through a series of dropping-off-my-father images the way you might step down on a sprained ankle to see if it's better when you know that really it's not. My father at the door to a hospital in Omaha, at a holistic health center in Iowa City, some mountain retreat with hot springs in northern Colorado, the ER in Kansas City, always with a look on his face like a child's.

When the boy gets up, I pull on the yellow terry-cloth shorts and the "I Left It All in Vegas" shirt from the gift shop and follow him to a suite on the floor just below the penthouse where the main space is unsurprisingly nine-tenths strippers and one-tenth businessmen. My mother and the grandfather are sitting on a sectional passing a bottle of tequila between them. Who is this person, I wonder?

"Drink?" the boy asks and thrusts a shot glass in my direction. I decide to take this as a command rather than a question and down it and then take another. It is then that my mother and the grandfather walk toward one of the suite's bedrooms and close the door. I can tell that my entire body is sunburned, and it hurts to lean back against the wall, but I do to steady myself, and the boy pushes his hips into mine and starts kissing me while moving me in the direction of the other open bedroom.

All the sex I've had has been strategically obliter-ating. It's never delicate, and it's never about feeling.

And this is no different. I am up against a beige wall next to a watercolor of a slot machine—a medium that doesn't quite fit the subject matter—and my shorts and swimsuit are around my ankles. The only real difference between this and the other obliterative sex in my past is that I'm fairly sure my mother is doing the same thing in the hotel bedroom adjacent to this one, which even without the timing would be something I'd prefer not to imagine.

When we finish and I know my back and elbows are scraped to shit and the boy is fanning his hair aside with his fingers and we are both quiet enough to hear the air conditioner cycle on, I pull my clothes up and walk out of the bedroom, past the strippers and the businessmen, down in the elevator where a woman in a teal cocktail dress puts on more mascara, past the front desk where a troupe of Realtors is checking in for a convention, and out of the lion entrance and onto the street. It's night but still ninety degrees, and of course every group is a bachelor party. I'm still in the gift store clothes, and I'm pretty sure I look like a runaway or a tourist, either of which could really fit, and I'm suddenly nothing but angry at my parents, those giant loping children, all need and ineptitude and no restraint.

It's Vegas, so of course there are lights and glowing signs everywhere I look: Silver City, Circus Circus, Enter the Night. If I were a different kind of person, I'd get onto a waiting bus to see where it would take me, but the fact is I'll end up in my mother's car the next morning driving west and hearing the details of the night before that I should not and will not want to hear.

I round the corner, and there's a man in front of a parking lot next to a diner getting punched repeatedly by another man. Both of them are in uniform shirts, and the man getting hit just takes it, over and over, and keeps standing. There's no circle of cheering people around them yelling, "Fight, fight, fight," like in a movie. Instead, everyone keeps walking past them, quickly, as if it isn't even happening.

For some reason I don't understand then and probably won't later, I run to their circle of motion and put myself between them, so close that I can see the bruising starting around the one man's eyes and the way he licks a drop of blood from the corner of his mouth.

"Hit me!" I yell to the one man. "Please."

At least I think I say it. At least I think I remember the punch landing and splitting the skin of my cheek. At least I think I remember driving all the way to the Pacific with my mother the next day with the windows mainly down and the music loud and a scab blooming across my face. At least I think I remember cupping saltwater and dipping my face into it so I could feel the sting. But maybe I didn't. Maybe I keep walking. Maybe I say nothing to no one. Maybe I get on a bus and sleep until Seattle or Billings. Who knows? None of this is familiar. None of this is anything like the world I have known.

THAT KIND OF LOVE

Melissa Llanes Brownlee

Tita imagines she is Pele, pouring herself under and through and over her island as she flings her silvery hair, draping it, strand by strand, over houses, cars, forests, rivers, the ocean. Tita loves to dig her toes into the sand of her special beach, a shimmering green crescent, sheltered by a high red cliff. She knows this sand is unique. It is not as rough as the black kind, with sunning sea turtles and buried lava rocks to stub your toe against, but it is not as smooth as the kind they ship in for the resorts. A perfect, soft white that coats her dark skin but brushes off so easily.

Here she feels connected to Pele, the goddess who falls in and out of love as the path of her lava changes. She understands this. How can anyone love just one person? She has loved three boys already this week, each as different as the sands on her island, her English, her math, her science notebooks filled with shifting initials in floating blue and black hearts. She also understands the raging jealousy of sharing lovers with others. She has seen it with her own parents, shouting matches about the past, *why you wen look at her I know you wen date him in high school you still like sleep with her,* echoing through the house after a wedding, a graduation party, a baby luau, but Tita believes it's something created by stupid men who felt the need to explain why Pele's lava flowed in particular places. Like a supernatural force needs a reason to do anything.

This beach is wild like her, a cove where people can get pulled out to sea before anyone notices, their yells for help buried in the crashing waves. Tita believes that Pele was drawn to this place. She believes that the god of this cove was as crazy as Pele and the sand is what became of this crazy love before they both went their separate ways. She knows that kind of love. She sees it in her parents, in her mother shredding her clothes in rage, packing up the car in the middle of the night, in her father punching holes in walls, emptied beer bottles following. She feels it in herself every day as her mind wanders in her classes, her daydreams filled with soft hands and softer kisses.

She would never be so stupid as to swim so far out as to risk the undertow and riptide, the ocean swallowing her screams, but she dreams of the day when she's not paying attention and finds herself drifting outside her cove, her feet dangling above the mile-high drop-off, the water so dark, the deep calling, and she thinks of the creatures waiting below, their tentacles wrapping around her, caressing, pulling her down into the depths, her special beach teasing her, glinting green in the distance.

HOW TO REVERSE TIME WHEN YOU'RE TIRED OF BEING THE HERO

Amber Sparks

XI

The return is the most difficult part; the thin membrane that separates the world from the quest is harder than diamonds. The hero pushes, he leans, he tries to reorder his atoms in the shape of a shepherd, a monk, a maiden. He slips through the world barrier sideways, but his sword catches on the air and shatters the calm into pieces. The townspeople whisper and bring him T-shirts and photos to sign; the hero smokes a cigarette and tries to look casual. His heart is already hurting for the high grasslands, the mysterious marshes, the dark forests with demons to catch and trails to follow. His heart is already beating faster in the slowness of the world.

X

The wound in his side smells rotten, stinks like death. He lies on his back like Prometheus, chained by pain and exhaustion. He watches the hawks circle overhead and thinks of his love, of the gold in her voice and hair, her hot pink toenails pushing into his calf while he tries to shake her awake from her nightmare. Her breasts soft round peaches in satchels. He groans and tries to rise, but stars rush to his eyes and he falls back. Dirt mixes with blood and pus. Hot winds blow through him, and he gropes for his cell phone. He needs a rescue. It is the truth, in the end: all heroes need rescuing after the quest is through. All heroes fall into themselves like empty clothes when the aim stops burning, when the last light has left the lining of their throats and they begin to be ordinary again.

IX

They ride out of hell with their prize held high. Swords out, car windows down, they sweep inevitable as locusts through wild, through wind, through wet and ocean that would drown a dead man. They fly faster than angels, as just in their cause. But they are followed by the stink of fear, by hurt, because they are only human, strange and soft a thing as that can be. Shields hard, they flee because they cannot fight. Swords high, they flee because they will die, but not yet. Not yet not yet today.

VIII

And there, in the clearing filled with light, the ultimate boon. It glitters flat, scratched and faded, this odd plain object of their quest. So much blood has soaked the ground in the seeking for it. The gods have starved in hunger for it. Heroes have shed their lives for it, villains paid whole souls for it; all the while no one wondering what will become of the world when it is found. No one wondering where the rain will fall, if all the tables are heavy with plenty and the soldiers as gentle as lambs.

VII

At the top of the tower, a mirror. A face glowering back in the dim light, heavy-browed and dark with shame. A prophecy of doom, of twin destroying twin, son murdering father. The fields are on fire outside. The burning crops smell like late fall back in the town, like the homecoming bonfires, like the children's stray voices, begging a penny for the Guy. Like closed eyes and deep breaths. Like the womb.

VI

Things that will tempt you to stray from the path: a woman, a battle, a bag of gold, a sword, a gun, a stack of jeans, a powder brick, a crown, a letter, a baseball, a pipe, a half-pipe, a fortune-teller's tell, a green monster, a monstrous ambition, a starring role, a huge breakfast, a bottle of wine, a bed and a fire and a very good book. The hammock your dad strung between the two big oak trees; the space that he made for you where his knees drew in, when you were so small you could press your whole face into one rope square and watch the ground swaying, swinging up to meet you again and again.

V

It doesn't really matter who she is, whether wife, mother, sister, aunt, grandmother, stepmother, goddess, saint, faerie, queen, angel. The point of her appearance is to give them respite, to vary the pace and to provide a dream for reference. Later, when they are tired as earth, when they are hungry as fire, when thoughts are murky and dark as the great ocean depths—the dream will give them succor. Later, the dream will give them strength. When back on their feet, sword in hand, they will worship but not understand the lady. They won't understand that she is stronger than warriors, for her strength is endless and boundless. They won't understand that she needs no weapons—only this vast reservoir of dream to draw upon, to bottle up and distribute to wandering heroes. They will brush this great gift from their boots like dust at the end of the day, and she will not mind. She is made for this fate, after all. She is the world's loveliest vending machine.

IV

Head out the door and stop for a moment; notice the copse of trees to your left and the town on your right. Remember how far you've never been before, notice the dead trees among the living and hope this is not a bad omen. Shudder slightly. Turn right. Find the dark magician in his foreclosed exurban home, and do battle. If you survive, leave the house and take the second left. Drive twenty miles to the nearest gas station and while you are filling up, find a tearful old lady who begs you to catch the thief who stole her purse. Explain that you are not the police and that you are on a quest, but feel so sorry for the old woman, who reminds you of your grandmother back home, that you give chase anyway. Catch the thief, who turns out to be a servant of the dark magician. Find out from him where his boss's lair is now located. At the first fork in the road, take a right. Drive ten miles through darkening, dense air and roll up your windows when the smog starts to push in. Continue to drive, seeking the lair but lost, mapless, blind, unsure what to do or where to go and positive you've made all the wrong choices. Blame the old lady, blame the thief, blame your father for not stopping you and your girlfriend for urging you on. Cry like a girl. Be glad no one can see you, but of course this is a quest and so everyone can see you. Everyone is watching. Everyone is waiting for you to get on with it. Get on with it.

III

Wizards use many weapons with varying degrees of proficiency, but do not use armor or shields. A wizard casts spells, which must be chosen ahead and prepared ahead of time. A wizard need not be strong, but a wizard must possess intelligence, and rest well before casting spells. A wizard may purchase a familiar, to assist him with magical tasks and provide companionship. A wizard may also present magical boons and tokens to help the hero on his journey, if the wizard so chooses. The wizard may not interfere with the hero's quest in any other way, though out of love and loyalty the wizard may choose to say the hell with it, and join the hero in saving the world or doing his best to try.

II

It starts with a stranger, or a close friend, but never a casual acquaintance. There must be something impassioned about the relationship, a love or a danger or both. There must be something to prove to this messenger, this strange herald who is unable to take up the task and must pass it on to another. Fate must choose, or judgment must choose, or love must choose, or all three in conjunction with the right or wrong planets. The new hero must be very lucky, or very unlucky, or perhaps he does not believe in luck at all. Perhaps he has already decided, long ago, that if such an offer were made he would grab at the chance. Perhaps he has sought such an offer. Perhaps he has fastened his hopes tight to this day, has kept watch for the moment when his best friend's eyes, or the stranger's eyes, or his father's or uncle's or brother's eyes move heavenward, just slightly, before coming to rest on the hero's ready shoulders at last.

I

The hero who is not yet the hero sits on a hill near the pasture, thinking of brighter things than cows and corn. He fills his dreams with sports cars, with travel, with books that look different from the books here and women who look different from the women here. He flicks his lighter, tips his cigarette with fire. He sighs to see his father approaching. The day will be ordinary, he supposes, like every day. The day will be chores, will be one big chore to forget and resume tomorrow.

The hero who is not yet the hero watches his father and worries he is starting to resemble the old man. He worries his life will be tedium, corn and cows, bills, endless mouths to feed, worry lines etched deep into a sun-spotted brow. But he doesn't worry too much; he changes the channel in his head and thinks of his girlfriend's hair, bright gold in the sun and sparkling like champagne. Of her eyes, blue and round as marbles. Of her breasts, downy and small. He thinks he could stick around for breasts like those.

He smiles and takes a last drag, grinds the cigarette butt into the soft dirt, watches the sun creep up into the sky, little by little. He thinks, yes, it would be worth it, to stick around here for breasts, for his father, for sunrises like these. For the beginnings of days to cycle back around and renew themselves, warm as embers, familiar already as home on the day he came into this world.

HIVE MIND

Melissa Bowers

T he mothers are coated in a light layer of fuzz, but only the children have ever noticed. As babies, it was a velvet comfort, hazy and unremembered—a soft place to rest while nursing or feverish or falling asleep. Now it's embarrassing. Devri and her friends complain to each other via text: *would it kill them to just fucking shave?*

*

Lila's mother is someone important—an astrophysicist who develops theories about quantum mechanics and tutors students for free.

Peyton's mother is someone important—an English professor at Stanford with six books and countless scholarly bylines.

Meg's mother is someone important—a person who scrubs other people's toilets, cooks other people's meals, folds other people's clothes.

But when they are seen, if they are seen at all, only one title matters. That's fine, they say if anybody asks. I am someone's mother, this is who I am, and I am finefinefinefinefine.

*

Before Devri's mother leaves for her interview—a profile on national TV because she is someone important, an entomologist or a melittologist or whatever—she kisses Devri on the corner of her mouth. "We'll be discussing the necessity of pollination," she says, joyous and assured, and Devri is proud of her, even though that horrifying downy skin will be magnified in HD.

But once the cameras start rolling, no one talks much about pollination. Not really. Instead, before millions and millions of viewers, the news anchor asks, "We have to know: how *do* you mamas juggle it all? You're just such busy little bees."

Devri's mother smiles tightly and tucks away her notes.

*

In Life Science class, this is what the students learn: Bee colonies can establish a functional nest in approximately a month, sometimes less. They're intentional about choosing protective locations for their homes. They are efficient and smart and patient and tireless and also kind of disgusting, the way they chew up all that wax in their creepy mouths and spit it out again to mold those tiny, perfect, endless hexagons. Most worker bees will die within six weeks, the teacher says. Devri is struck by the relentless labor of a life so short, and wonders if they would change anything—if they know, or do not know, the specific brevity of their time here, if they would still choose to shoulder such a heavy load.

At the end of the unit there is a project that culminates in an oral report and one required hour of community service. Lila decides to stand in the cafeteria with a hand-drawn sign that says ♥SAVE THE BEEEEZ PLEEEEZ♥. Peyton plants black-eyed Susans in the courtyard. Meg distributes flyers to her neighborhood. Devri spends a whole morning volunteering with her mother, collecting samples, peering through microscopes, analyzing and charting movement patterns. For a few days they discuss the importance of a species they'd mainly ignored—"From now on, we must remember how absolutely crucial they are," Devri tells the class when she delivers her speech—but by the weekend, Lila is preoccupied with her girlfriend and Peyton's dad has started drinking again and Meg needs to study for her geometry final *or else*, and everyone, including Devri, forgets.

*

The first time her mother doesn't come home, no one pays much attention. Late night at work, Devri assumes, and never investigates further, even when her mother leaves for the grocery store the following Saturday and slips in the side door after dark—without groceries. Word spreads slowly, like an ooze: more and more they are missing, mothers who live down the street and across town and two states over, the mother who is supposed to host Lila when she studies abroad in Spain, the mother of Peyton's ex–best friend who moved to New Hampshire last summer, the mother of Meg's favorite K-pop star.

The last time Devri's mother comes upstairs to say good night, Devri does not know it will be the last time. She is half-asleep beneath a shower of fluttering kisses, on her forehead and on her cheeks and all over the backs of her hands, wordless, a honeyed smell lingering in the air even after she is gone.

*

Afterward, Devri will wonder how so many people could have missed it for so long: the way mothers everywhere tugged sweater sleeves around their wrists to conceal fresh stripes, the way they learned to hide antennae in their hair. She will wonder if anyone suspected what they were up to, and the whole world will say: No, we had no idea, how were we supposed to realize they were ready to escape?

But Lila will claim her mother's speech began to change—mostly Z's where S's should have been. Peyton will have nightmares about her mother's jaws. Meg will swear she watched wings unfurl. And Devri will recall a moment—just one singular moment, though she'll try to picture her mother all the ways she was, flitting around the kitchen, zipping up and down the stairs, hovering lovingly over her children—when she'd looked her in the eye and been hypnotized by mesmerizing, bulbous black orbs.

Some evenings, for comfort, Devri will play back the interview again and again, listen to the hum of that familiar voice.

"...*a collective awareness. A swarm intelligence. They share resources, knowledge, passed along to each other indefinitely, and together they know things the individuals do not.*"

It's no one's fault, everyone will say: We couldn't possibly have predicted what they were building, or why they would ever want to disappear. All we know is the devastation once it finally split open—colonies and colonies and colonies pouring from their honeycomb explosion, spilling toward freedom, stingers poised, having found a way to make a hive entirely of queens.

SURFACE TREATMENTS
Zach Powers

I t took less than a month for the coats of paint to completely cover the electrical outlet in the kitchen. So much for coffee. So much for toast. The nearest outlet was in the dining room. The longest extension cord was only six feet. We suggested that our parents buy a longer one, maybe one that wasn't orange and meant for outdoors, maybe one that wasn't caked with saffron dirt, but we were only children. Like most children, even the wisest things we said went ignored.

This was when Dad sometimes didn't work. This was when Mom sometimes didn't drink.

When Dad did work, it was part time, painting houses. We would ride to Waffle House, where they had toast, Dad pointing out decorative shutters on split-level ranch styles. That's Surfin', he would say of a pair painted blue. He had painted those and many shutters besides. The names never quite matched the colors. Dignified, Intuitive, Jovial, Reticence. Some were named with words we'd never heard of. Loggia, for example, which sounded like a word we would later learn but we would learn had no relation.

They let our dad keep the extra paint. "They" being his bosses, who hired him because he looked like the other men they hired, skin somewhere between Quinoa and Hopsack. We were all blond like Mom, at least like

49

Mom before she went early gray. Passive. Neither Mom nor Dad had emigrated from farther away than Ridgeland, South Carolina.

Whenever Dad had a day off from painting, he painted the kitchen walls. The first few times, we thought it normal. We had school friends who told us of the new colors their rooms had taken. Their colors were banal: pink, yellow, blue, green. We asked for specificity. They never knew what we meant.

That first month, Dad repainted the kitchen five times, and he painted it ten the next. In all the months that came after, he added fifteen fresh coats on average. On days Mom didn't drink, she would help Dad paint. On days she did, she would yell at Dad for always painting. Sometimes, she'd leave the house and come home hours later with her own half-empty containers, handles of whiskey with names as diverse as Dad's colors: Old Crow, Old Grand Dad, Kentucky Gentleman, Wild Turkey, Early Times.

We should say that Mom never yelled at us. With us she mostly hugged and cried, always at once.

First it was the power outlets, and then the layers of paint thickened to the width of the trim, the crown molding, the light switches. Mom switched to candles. A midwinter coat of Bolero, red like dried blood, stuck the faucet in the off position. After that, the bathroom sink provided our drinking water. We had to use the dishwasher for even the filthiest pots, but that was not long a worry. The stove's back console disappeared under paint a few weeks after the faucet.

Dad spent less time painting at work and more time painting at home. Mom opted for vodka, for economical reasons, she explained. Taaka her vodka of choice.

When she left the bathroom with a glass in hand, it was never clear whether it was water or not.

By Christmas, a coat of festive Kilkenny overlapped the lip of the counter. Mom and Dad had saved up enough to buy us each a Ninja Turtle. The turtles shared the names of famous painters, but we called them instead by the colors of their masks.

Soon the paint on the walls swelled beyond the kitchen cabinets, layering over them like sediment, sealing away their contents to await fossilization. Lost forever inside were colanders and mugs and whisks and forks and sponges and a drawerful of uncategorized junk.

Mom stopped entering the kitchen altogether. Dad left only to bathe and sleep and work.

The doorway shrank, growing more child-sized with every coat of paint. Dad had to enter sideways, ducking his head. Sometimes he added two coats a day. The fridge door drowned beneath a wash of Ebbtide. The oven melted into red-orange Emberglow.

Now it resembled less a kitchen and more a hall, though it led nowhere. That's when the gallon buckets could no longer fit through the door.

Dad had to stretch his arm back through the gap just to dip the brush's bristles in the paint. He put down old gray newspapers to protect the threshold from dribbles. He never crossed the threshold himself.

We cleaned Dad's brushes for him in the bathroom sink. Paint stink and toothpaste mint. We brought him protein bars, gummy things we couldn't stomach ourselves. He urinated in Solo cups and defecated in plastic Kroger bags, and we would take turns dumping the urine in the toilet, tossing the fetid bags in the backyard. We fetched new colors from the garage. Cans stacked in neat rows rose to the ceiling, crisscrossed by cobwebs, aisles for walking among them. Even on tiptoes, we could reach the tops of only the shortest columns. We could lift only cans more than half empty.

One day we delivered some sort of blue, the name of the color dripped over by the color itself. Mom slouched against the wall outside the kitchen. For months she had confined herself to other rooms. We had seen at most her shadow. Her hair now was stark white. She seemed asleep but stirred at our steps. We set down the can beside her.

She pried the can open with the blunt side of a splotchy knife and stirred the paint with the blade. We recognized it as Dad's old chef's knife, which Mom must have salvaged before it was entombed in a drawer.

Dad passed Mom a brush through the doorway, now just a gap as an archer might use in a castle. She plunged the brush deep into the can and smeared away the excess paint on the rim. She passed the brush back. We heard the wet rasp of Dad painting. The brush reemerged from within the kitchen. Mom reapplied paint, returned the brush through the gap.

Every morning Mom greeted us from that same spot on the floor. Every morning she clutched the chef's knife in her hand.

Weeks passed. We peeked through the doorway, now no wider than a thick coat of paint. A morning shaft of Goldfinch slanted inside, but it was too dim to reveal any details. Not that any details survived. Too dim, then, to identify the final color the kitchen had taken.

Mom pressed her lips to the crack. We thought we heard Dad whisper a reply, but it might have been the sound of the brush, painting his side smaller and smaller and smaller.

HELD UNDER

Kathleen McKitty Harris

My mother tells the story like this: she threw a glass of cold water in my five-year-old face while I was sleeping because an elderly neighbor, who'd read about the tactic in *Woman's Day,* had suggested it as a way to rouse me because I was utterly impossible to wake up in the morning; because it's what parents did back then and what did she know; because she was at her goddamn wit's end.

What she didn't say: she threw a glass of cold water in my five-year-old face because she and my father kept me up too late the night before playing poker at a friend's house in Weehawken, New Jersey, and she couldn't get my five-year-old body out of bed the next morning; because some distant drunk relative threw her into the rough Rockaways surf once when she was small and she couldn't swim, and the freezing ocean water shocked her into an awareness of her own mortality; because her grandmother had once held her own toddler head under the faucet too long while washing her brown bobbed hair in a chipped white enameled sink and she was traumatized by the water hitting her face and believed I should suffer the same fate; because my father drank too much Scotch and water and had crashed a car a few months earlier; because she was terrified of both staying and leaving; because her marriage and mind were in trouble; because she was afraid of drowning in a landlocked neighborhood and a loveless union in Queens.

When my mother recounted the incident that afternoon to a neighbor at the kitchen table, over cups of percolated coffee and a cloud of menthol cigarette smoke, their commingled laughter wafted down the hall to my bedroom. That sound of her mockery—that stinging shame of her amusement at my situation—is what made me decide to run away from home that day. This was after the ice-chilled liquid hit my face in a sudden, swift stream from tumbler to cheek; after she'd walked out of my room and I'd changed out of my soaked summer nightgown, balling it up in the recesses of my closet; after I'd sat on my bed and reprised the morning's events with my Holly Hobbie doll and her bonneted, brunette counterpart Heather; after I realized that something was very wrong with my mother.

I had one of those dime-store valises covered in cheap brocade fabric. We didn't travel much. I only used it for weekend sleepovers at both sets of grandparents' houses in Brooklyn and Queens. I took down the valise from my closet shelf and packed my teddy bear, two pairs of underwear, as many Little Golden Books as I could reasonably fit in the top zip pocket, my piggy bank laden with pennies and silver dollars, and a windbreaker, in case of inclement weather. The bulging valise made me look like a tiny carpetbagger on her way to seek financial gain in the Deep South.

My mother must have heard the commotion and entered my bedroom, asking me what I was doing.

I'm packing, I said. *I'm running away from home.*

My mother was confused and flustered. I couldn't do that. What did I mean by that?

She hurried back to the kitchen to tell her friend. They both stood dumbfounded as I walked past, valise in hand.

Where are you going? My mother asked me.

Africa, I answered. Because it was the furthest place from her that I could think of.

My mother ran out after me. *At least wait until your father gets home to say goodbye. Just sit on the stoop and wait until he gets home.*

I figured I owed him the courtesy, so I did. For more than an hour. I didn't budge. The neighbor left, wished me well on my journey.

Then my father walked down the street from the Myrtle Avenue bus stop, smelling of Scotch and cigarettes and sweat and everyone else who rode the express coach from midtown Manhattan.

You're running away? He said to me calmly, as my mother cried inside the house. He placed his oxblood-loafered foot on the brick stoop beside me, stretching his bent leg like a runner warming up his muscles before a sprint.

Yep, I answered, watching as the lit end of his Marlboro flared with his inhale.

I see, he said. *Where ya headed?*

Africa, I said.

How much money yuh got?

I don't know, I said. *I brought my whole piggy bank.*

That won't get even get you into the city, he told me. *Forget about getting a cab to JFK. Forget about a plane ticket. You wanna come inside and talk about this some more?*

There was something crossing his face that I'd never seen before. A smirk, a ripple of emotion. Newfound respect for me, maybe. A sameness of purpose. We both knew something was seriously wrong here. I didn't know then that he wanted to run away, too.

He walked me back into our apartment, and my valise went back in the closet. We didn't talk about it some more. We just moved on, with our pain and our mistakes and our sadness stored away as well.

I never tried to run away again, but instead, became embedded and enmeshed in the tumult of our family. I was marooned on their island, parched for normalcy, for a semblance of a happy childhood, for an example of a loving partnership between husband and wife. But help never arrived in those years, not for any of us.

More than thirty years later, my father packed his own bag. He got sober, told me she'd been *holding him under* all this time. He served my mother divorce papers, and ran away from both of us. I haven't spoken to him in years.

I tell the story like this: My parents divorced when I was thirty-six. It could have been worse. It wasn't like they split up when I was a kid and I had to shuttle back and forth between apartments, between bedrooms at her place and his. I was an adult. I was married with kids of my own. I had it easy, really. It wasn't like I was a kid when it happened. You know?

What I don't say: I was a kid when it happened, that five-year-old girl wanting to run from my mother, still wanting to be free of her madness and the umbilical cord she refuses to sever; still getting in my car when the argument goes too far and I can't find my way to resolution; still finding myself on the highway at night with the Stones blasting on my radio, still wanting to be anywhere but in my own skin; still looking for my father to say what he never does, which is *I stayed for you I wanted you I wanted to be your father I still want to be your father.*

A GOOD RUN OF IT

Edie Meade

I

The sun sets for hours when you drive west. I pretend to live on another planet, tangerine tinging alien outlet malls, electric substations, in the rearview the sweating peach-flesh of my kids, junkyards and flooded fields and on into another god's country, all asleep, all peaceable. On another planet I would be grateful for providence because I could believe, I think, in a god responsible for daiquiri rain. Or a god not responsible for all the stupid suffering we go through. Let's get us away from here, babies, and pretend there's a benevolent god somewhere in the universe, shimmering the air with happiness.

Gradually the sky draws down milky purple, and a few smoky clouds sigh out the last of the orange with me, and the boys' heads stop rolling on their car seats and they go to sleep so soundly I wonder if they can breathe with their necks like that and if they'll ask where Daddy is when they wake up. And then we turn south and I know I'm reconciling with the same planet as always, with the same physics, where I can only drive so far, so fast, so long toward the only possible god who sets low, glaring red before me.

*

Nashville motel, third floor. Me and the kids. No vacancy
for hours around, some March Madness thing? I don't
follow sports, or anything, really. I unpack the kids
one at a time honking the car lock each trip like I'm
worried about a true-crime kidnapping; maybe I'm the
kidnapper; maybe the Amber Alert is coming. I carry
the little one and kick at stray parking lot gulls gusted
in from the river.

    We got in here somehow, cash-through-Plexiglas
crack of dawn. All smoking rooms with single beds
with dips like shallow graves in the middle. I guess
we're good if this chair can brace the door shut. Over
a decrepit fence, club lights bounce purple, red, colors
of almost emergency over the bazooka bass screams of
almost chaos spilling red into the lot, into the crack of
the almost open door. I'm so tired. So tired. Tired. I sleep
asthmatic, cycling with the wall unit, cadaver-straight
between the kids.

2

No coffee, why do I do this to myself? In lieu of gas
station coffee, a dirt of nothing. My own hot teeth, mule-
tongue sleepy. Still no shit. I'm too sober to feel this hung
over. Morning clubbers have fallen to the cackling of
parking lot starlings. On the wall a montage of Nashville
neon BBQ signage as though everything is fine. The
lot puddles. Soggy masks, oil, jellyfishing convenience
store bags. I watch my step for syringes. Force of habit.
I still love him. I can find something in anything.

    On the main road, another neon, a road crew of men
I know I have already caressed in other lives, miserable,
laying down hot mix, rolling their smell to me. Dawn

pinks them up but they're unimpressed by bouquets. It's not beauty mankind is after, after all. It's too cold, too early for all of this. They work under their own light, focused and intense and oblivious to me up here on the balcony, yearning or mourning, feeling something about their man shapes under their safety vests. I remember the heft of his boots. And I'm glad, at least, to be alive.

3

Day three. The kids are done with it. We dogleg down Alabama into wild flats, take the high road into low country. Montgomery, a place almost as beautiful and hurt as West Virginia. We break to eat a Little Caesars Hot-N-Ready on the curb of a parking lot and the boys learn about fire ants. Their shoes are already heavy with sand two hundred miles from the beach. I flick a black ant the size of a northern wasp off the littler boy's ear before he panics. Panic comes with recognition and he is innocent. Isn't this fun? We're going to the beach. Do you know how much sand is at the beach? There are no ants at the beach, I tell them and hope it's true because I've never been to a real beach. I hope we can make it to the beach, without knowing what we will do after that.

Spiders web the gap of my window at the stoplight, the industry of panhandlers. I fight back, hurl them away, feel guilty, greet in my motion the woman at the corner. She flings, too, in a hallucinatory grip with her own devils. I telegraph my own aspirations to her as the light changes: I want you to win.

*

How could she go back to him? Everyone will ask forever. I guess there's humanity in the what-ifs. We're always imagining an escape, if not for ourselves then for others. We had a good run of it, didn't we? But we're bottoming out, March Madness, march to the sea. I'm out of money. The geography of money is a basin, I think. I don't know how to turn around on my own, never have, so I'll let the Gulf do it for me.

The Gulf isn't even the ocean; it's just a basin of the sea. I feel so hollow. But we're here. We made it every bit as far as I swore I would drive. Now I'm sitting in my rolled-up jeans on the sand at the edge of the world, not thinking about what's next, just thinking about the way his eyelids purple up when he's emotional but how I've never seen him actually cry. This is the first time I've ever seen the sun set over water. The truth is the sun never stops setting because we just keep on moving. Let the kids have a day at the beach, let them know what it's like to run with the wind for a little while. The sunset just goes and goes, my god. If there was a real god, it would look just like this.

IN THE COMPANY OF SADIE STAR

Jamy Bond

We dip our hands into our father's jean pockets, searching for Viceroys to tuck into our training bras. We prefer our mother's Eve cigarettes, but she hides them better. Hers come in a package with pastel flowers that swirl like hair around a woman's porcelain face. We feel pretty when we smoke them.

There are no cigarettes in any of our father's pockets, but there are Polaroids. A stack of three, the same scene from different angles: a woman spread out on our parents' orange bed, red fingernails slipping into pink wetness, a gaudy gold ring on one finger. Those fingernails and that ring belong to Sara's mom. She lives across the street and smokes mentholated Kools: each puff feels like a winter breeze going down.

We steal the Polaroids and run out the back door, deep into the woods, and we do not stop until all we see are dense, green patches of trees stretching into a gray sky.

These woods are mysterious and beautiful and sometimes they surprise us. Once we found a dilapidated cabin that seemed to materialize out of thin air. We broke in through a window and stayed for hours, relishing in the dirt and stink of the place. What freedom to know that our mother wasn't around to clean it until her fingers bled. We lounged on dusty bunk beds and posed questions to our Magic 8 Ball, shaking it briskly, waiting for the answers to appear in its black triangular sea.

"Is our father possessed by the devil?"

It is decidedly so.

"Should we perform an exorcism?"

Better not tell you now.

"If our mother runs away, will she take us with her?"

Don't count on it.

We hop the creek and dart some bramble bushes and find Sara sitting with her back against a tree trunk. Sometimes she steals cigarettes from her aunt Marie, who lives in the basement. Marie smokes More cigarettes, our favorites, long and slender and the color of chocolate. When we smoke them, we feel like the woman in the More advertisements we've seen in our mother's *Cosmopolitan* magazine, pushing a buttery leg through a thigh-high slit in a black evening gown, wearing pointy-toed heels with diamond-studded ankle straps, holding a delicate cigarette between pale fingers and smirking at the camera because we know a secret, because we DARE TO BE MORE.

"Hey Sara," Beth says. "Got any Mores for us?"

"Not today," she says, without looking our way. "And you can call me Sadie."

"Sadie?"

"Yes. Sadie Star."

She pulls a More from behind her ear and taps it against her wrist.

"But your name is Sara," I say, "Sara Sanchez."

"Not anymore," she says and presses the cigarette between her lips. She pulls a silver Zippo from her jean pocket and flips it open with the flick of her wrist.

"Have you gone nuts?" I ask.

"You're lucky to be in the company of Sadie Star," she says and looks out at the place where a bridge made of rotting wood and dangling ropes crosses a wide place in the creek.

"We found some dirty pictures in our father's closet," Beth says. "Wanna see them?"

She holds out her hand. "I guess."

Beth gives her the pictures and we both look away, up at the darkening sky.

After a glance, Sara tosses them in the dirt.

"Sadie Star isn't interested in *that*," she says. "Sadie Star is interested in freedom."

"Freedom," I say.

She forms a circle with her lips and pops out perfectly round smoke rings that drift into the air like misty halos.

"Can we have one?" Beth asks.

"No. Sadie Star needs to conserve the rest."

She looks out at the bridge again. Beyond it, the trees thin out and a muddy field stretches as far as the eye can see. When summer comes, a rainbow of wildflowers will fill that space.

"Do you want to see something?" Sara asks, standing up. She drops her cigarette in the dirt and crushes it with her boot.

We act like we don't, but we do and she knows it.

"You'll have to turn around and close your eyes."

We moan and snort and snicker, and then we do it.

"You'll have to put your hands up in the air."

"That's bogue," Beth says.

"Just do it. Do it for Sadie Star," she says.

So we do it, because whatever Sara has to show us, we know it's a billion times more interesting than anything we've got waiting at home. I can hear her footsteps in the leaves coming around the side of me and moving to the front.

"Okay," she says. "Ready."

When we open our eyes, she is standing before us with a small, silver gun in her hand. It looks fantastic and shiny and real.

"Where'd you get that?" I ask as a small anchor of worry grips my chest.

"I stole it from Paula."

Ever since she found out she's adopted, she calls her mom Paula instead of Mom.

"What are you going to do with it?" Beth asks.

"Sadie Star needs protection," she says.

For a moment I see her like she wants me to, without the yellow teeth and Coke-splattered T-shirt, those muddy boots and ripped-up jeans. Sadie Star. I see her in the summer sun, running through that field of wildflowers, and all I want is to be running too.

"Wherever you're going," I want to ask her, "can we go along?" But before I can get the words out, she fires the gun. The sound ricochets off the trees and fills the sky, so loud, I can feel it inside of me. I see Beth from the corner of my eye, fluttering around in a panic, but when I open my mouth to speak, nothing comes out.

A strange ache pulses deep in my belly—thump, thump, thump—and darkness rolls in like moss.

SUDDENLY, A MAN

Hananah Zaheer

T he photo station at Eckerd had been calling for two weeks to *please pick up if you don't want your memories destroyed.*

It might cheer everyone up to see pictures, Abba figured, since sitting around in a hospital room for weeks was no fun, not when your only daughter's jaw was wired shut and her eyes puffed up and sticky just like that phullee rice she used to secretly buy from the rehri-wallah in Pakistan—*remember her spirit?* Amma kept saying and *do something* and he kept feeling useless, not knowing what it was they all wanted from him. No one knew exactly what misstep had landed her in that bed in the first place—everyone kept being curt with him like it was his fault, like it was he who had driven her to Asheville in the middle of the night, no word to anyone, then told her to call Amma, saying she had decided not to have a baby and they could keep her husband and his degree, she was never coming back—though Nani, who had been considering death more than the others, knew women ended up in all kinds of beds for all kinds of reasons, and wondered if there would be any waking up at all.

I'm going to the pharmacy, he said, but everyone ignored him and kept talking about *when she wakes up, so stressful now, a whole court case.*

He took the Nissan, ignoring the dented hood from
when his son-in-law drove it into the window of their
house not even an hour after he had called the boy to
let him know she was back and all was okay, straight
into the dining table where her mother and her aunt
were standing above her saying *motherhood is a beautiful thing* why did she not tell them did she not have
their family's respect in mind had they not given her
everything she wanted, and wondering if it really was
some sense of morality, and not fear of his relatives'
opinions, that had made him call his son-in-law to come
get her—*what else would a man do with his grief when
his wife runs away?* the son-in-law had said to the police,
*she's not been raised right she is a whore she doesn't know
how to make me happy she killed our baby she's having an
affair, that fucking bitch*—and drove down Horton and
up Duke and parked in the handicap spot—habit—and
strode to the photo counter, daughter's phone in hand
to show them the messages they kept leaving on her
voicemail, irritation in his voice.

You should not bother your customers so much, he
said. *Maybe they're already having to stop from wanting
to kill someone. Maybe they are trying not to die.*

He was so frazzled that he nearly ripped the bottom
of the envelope when they handed it to him. *That should
show them how not okay it is*, he thought.

She had been smoking for years, but you could not
find a single picture of her holding a cigarette so it
was a hungama—*haey Allah*, Nani kept wailing even
though no one was listening—when Abba handed that
one photo to Amma saying *dekho lo*. In the picture she
was leaning against a balcony against a backdrop of
mountains, holding a cigarette in her lips. She had a

defiant look on her face, like she was daring the camera to do something about it, looking exactly like Abba had feared her looking when they first arrived in America, when his own father and his friends and everyone had said *don't take your young daughter there, you don't know what those countries do to them, what kind of a man are you*—a kind of hatred and a wildness on her face.

He called her mother into the hallway immediately. *Did you know she smokes? What else does she do?* he asked, angry at his wife now because she must have known something—mothers always know things about their daughters—and he expected he would have to get loud enough for her to confess, but she said no she did not and the shocked way she said it sounded true, though his skin felt hot, and he felt like he needed the sharp sting of someone's face against his own palm.

They passed the picture around the hospital room. Nani, her mother and aunt were trying to come up with reasons why she might do this.

Maybe it was a prop, her mother said. *Maybe she was in a play.* Kids in college were in plays, she had heard, and her daughter did have a tendency to be dramatic, fighting about every small rule. The fuss she had made when Abba found her a husband, saying she could never get married without getting a degree first—lucky she was beautiful, and had not ruined her chances working at convenience stores and hotel desks like the Khan girls who had also moved to America same year as them—as if she didn't come around at the end herself when she saw how handsome he was.

What play would she be in? Nani said, thinking that the boy—new husband—was far too serious to let her go hang around with strangers for hours. He hadn't lived long enough to know what mattered, what to let go of. Fancy degree and fancy doctor's coat, but no culture, no sense of adventure. His brain was all wrong. They really shouldn't have made her marry him, not so quickly anyway, but who could bother listening to an old woman, especially if she was saying *I told you* so and the evidence was hooked up to oxygen machines for all to see.

The monitors kept up the steady beep in the hospital room while the women bent over the photo, trying to figure out what might have possessed her to take a picture like this.

Maybe she is just posing for the picture. Aunt looked closely at the photo. *I don't see a lighter. I don't see smoke.*

Maybe, Amma said. *Maybe she was just trying to get our attention.*

Maybe it's just a phase.

Maybe she was only trying to make a point.

I hear they have candy cigarettes.

She will stop.

She's a good girl.

Everything will be fine.

Her father stood beside the bed, arms crossed, staring at her face, looking at the fingers that had held the cigarette. He was wondering what kind of other things she had held, what went through her head, who it might have been that took that picture, what other things did he not know about her, suddenly believing that maybe he understood his son-in-law a little bit after all.

Maybe, Nani said, looking at him, not saying the other things she was thinking.

The daughter's coma was deep. She could not hear any of the conversation. She could not know what they were thinking. But before the car came crashing in the window, she had been rolling the disposable camera between her palms, thinking her father was never going to understand her after all, she was never going back to her husband, and she would never bend to anyone's will again.

TRANSFORMISTA

aureleo sans

f I can't smuggle in Bernice and Ra Ra, there's no way I'm going to win Haven for Hope's first annual talent show and I want grand prize more than anything. It's an airboat tour of the Everglades.

They told us, "We are trying to broaden your horizons," and while I don't know about all that and I don't know what an evangelical tour is, like is baby Jesus going to float down the swamp in a basket and we'll have to take turns bobbing for him?, what I do know is nature speaks to me, specifically seabirds, and I heard the Fountain of Youth is somewhere in the park and maybe we could find it and my mom told me once that our people came from the swamp and maybe I'll meet a long-lost relative because dreams do happen. But first I've got to gain entrance.

"What do you mean you are banning my little friends?"

I stare hard at Shirley. I can't stand fuckin' gatekeepers. I don't tell her that. She sniffs twice. Sniff, sniff. She should be banned. Snorting lines of coke in the community bathroom is not only unprofessional but it's a violation of the rules.

"Sir, as we told you last week, you cannot come into the shelter with wild animals on your shoulder or barely concealed in your coat."

Bernice squints her possum eyes.

"She's treating us like vermin, man. Does she think I am a ratchet rat?" Bernice's clicking was starting to get elevated. She was the feisty one, and I was trying to avoid riling her up so I continued with Shirley.

"But what about Brownie?"

"Haven for Hope has a policy to allow service dogs like Brownie. Opossums are not service animals."

"That vest was bought off Craigslist and everybody knows it!" I start flapping my hands at her. (It's true that Brownie's owner claims to be blind, but how come he's always looking in the right direction?)

Sniff, sniff, snort, sniff, sniff. I question the safety of Shirley's nostrils.

"Did she even have a septum left?" I scribble furiously in the spiral notebook I tote around like destiny. It is how I interpret the world.

I write: "The color of Shirley's force field was vermilion. It flickered in tandem with each sniff." From an early age, I could detect force fields. These weren't protective bubbles like you see in the comics, but rather they enveloped people in shafts of light shooting skyward. They didn't protect the person. They elucidated the telltale heart. The warmer the color, the darker the shade.

"But I need them for the show. It's for my big reveal!" The start time for the show is ticking closer and I had a lip sync performance to Stacey Q's "Two of Hearts" all mapped out. My competitor and ex-boyfriend, Toribio, had been eyeing my possums all week as he Elmer-glued wads of chewed-up bubble gum to his scalp that kept falling off and sticking to residents' shoes.

I try a new tack. "He's the one who should be banned,"

I yell, pointing at Toribio's busted mug. Except for her nose, Shirley is unmoved.

This had been a rough homecoming. Two days had passed since I left the Bexar County Jail and my lover Fernando. The jail warehoused faggots like us like we were species of prey at the zoo that had to be separated from the predators. They called it "the gay wing." But I didn't care why the caged bird sings. We weren't prey. We had penises.

Two days had passed, and my heart ached for *RuPaul's Drag Race*. Every Friday night we crowded into the TV room to watch the latest episode. I started flipping through drawings in my spiral and on the runway chasséd panthers, piscine succubi in wheelchairs, swallowtails on stilts, and beetles that pranced.

My favorite sketch: During the Death Becomes Her runway, Katya wore a sequined captain's outfit as the lemon shark gnawed at her knee stump. Of course, I observe at the meth-addled altar of Katya. Like her, I am a recovering friend of Tina. Locked up, I realized all my life I have been sick and tired of being sick and tired. But drag reflected the verve of the life I always knew. What everyone else had denied. What everyone else had denied me.

"Please leave. The shelter cannot permit the entrance of flea-infested wildlife into this facility. We will not abide pestilence," Shirley mumbles. She sniffs.

Bernice flashes teeth. Bernice hisses and screams, "We eat fleas, motherfucker!"

Shirley swipes at her desk. She fumigates Bernice. Bernice drops to the floor. She skitters home. The vermilion deepens. Blood beads. Ra Ra feigns death. Shirley shrieks.

"That motherfucking bitch bit my nose!"

The shelter audience roars.

Let me tell you a joke. If I catch a charge, can I throw it back?

Another one: Sometimes where you live isn't always a home.

The shelter manager, a willow tree of a man, delivers me outside. Tells me I made the list of "undesirable residents" again. In my hurry to avoid law enforcement, I leave Ra Ra in the supine position. As I zigzag run, I zigzag write: "When no shelter will shelter you, when every refuge refuses you, when no one recognizes your humanity, who are you?"

I've been told by doctors that I'm "not an accurate historian," that I'm a "storyteller," which when translated in doctorspeak means "malingerer." But they all are wrong. I am a fabulist.

Once after a visit to the mental ward, I requested my medical records. They took three months to arrive. The most hurtful thing I read was the doctors described my nose as a "proboscis." I prefer the term "aquiline." They noted the impossibility of my legs. Long ago, HIV stole my calves and quadriceps.

I lope on stilted legs from the shelter to an abandoned field five blocks away. At the thrift store for veterans, I discovered a carnation pink dress, the type Laura Bush would wear. It feels bunched below the middle. I should have tucked. No time now. I need to finish the look, and I reach into my pocket for a pair of shears.

Harvesting thistle blooms, the color of thirsty tongues, looks more dangerous than it is. They call thistle a noxious weed. I smoke noxious weed. They call me a noxious weed. Am I a noxious weed?

Prickles—what a word!—cover the plant from root to flower. The flower itself looks dangerous, each petal a sharpened blade ready to maim, but I'm not so easily hoodwinked. In reality, they wilt with too much handling and so with care I lop the thistle into four Walmart grocery bags until the bags overflow with decapitated blooms.

A round hooker had gifted me two vials of eyelash adhesive and a wispy pink wig, cotton candy delicate. She said she didn't need them anymore for her "vocation." She was giving it up. She was giving up the light. I told her I didn't know about all that but I mopped her beauties anyway.

I place the wig on my head. I tell the world, "You should see me in this crown," and then I cover my face, legs, and arms with the adhesive and then I cover my face, legs, and arms with the thistle.

I transform into a flamingo. I honk. I gabble. I fly away.

TIMES HE TOUCHED HER IN THE NIGHT

Aubrey Hirsch

L ot's hands on her shoulders, when he wakes her to tell her it's time to run. The world comes into focus around her: first the red of the clay walls, then the sounds of her sleeping daughters breathing in unison, the smell of oil, the heat of her swelling cheek. Just after her pleasant dream of soft, fresh grass, and just before her mouth fills with salt, she doesn't recognize his touch. She tries to remember the last time she'd woken to the feel of his skin on hers, but fails.

Before that it was Lot's knuckles across her cheekbone. He'd been entertaining men, as he often did, but this time he didn't want to share. When the others came, he tried to offer their daughters instead. She stood in front of the door, weeping. She watched his hand grow through the puddle of her tears.

She searches her memory, a haunted labyrinth. Before that it must have been the birth of their second daughter. Lot forced her knees apart, refused to look at her. When she wiped the bloody handprints from her thighs there were bruises underneath.

Before that was the night he put the baby inside her. Lot had come home drunk, smelling like the sweat of other men. She still had hope that there was love for her inside him, but if there was, he gave no hint of it. He touched her ankle, she lifted her eyes to his, then he flipped her face down on the sleeping mat, forcing himself roughly inside her only to finish. She could just make out his footsteps moving toward the door under the sound of their older daughter crying.

Before that it was the birth of their first, the last time he touched her with tenderness. The memories of the pain are vivid but so are these: Lot wiping sweat from her brow, Lot rubbing her feet, Lot's lips on her shoulders. There were women to help, but Lot wanted to watch the baby come. She never dreamed the shift in his expression from love to revulsion could be so quick, or so permanent.

Before that, she's almost sure, though there's no way to prove it now, there was hugging and kissing and intertwining of fingers. Before that, there was the smell of Lot in her hair. Before that, the heavy weight of his arm across her belly in the dark. Before that, the throbbing of his chest against hers when he pulled her close. And before that, the first time he touched her in the night, after the wedding, when she was scared and pretended to be sleeping and he ran a fingertip from her forehead to her chin so slowly she thought the moment would never end, then lay down beside her, and through the smallest possible opening of her eyelids, she saw him smile.

And now he is telling her to run. Lot tells her her home is no longer her home. He says the men he brought home are really angels. The smell of his breath could kill a sheep. The same daughters he tried to sacrifice only hours ago, he tells her now, he is trying to save.

Lot has packed a small bag with food, clothes, a water skin. He drags her through the door still blinking with sleep. "Don't look back," he says. All she can think about are the things behind her: her sleeping mat, her mother's necklace, the little wooden birds she carved for her daughters, the cloth she wrapped them in when they were new, their collection of speckled stones and owl feathers and walnut shells. "Don't look back," he says again, so she looks at Lot's hair and his sweaty neck. His skin is red from drink and sex and fear.

Lot says, "Don't look back," but in front of her there is only the culmination of all of her nightmares. She closes her eyes, but she stumbles and trips. She looks at the ground. Her shadow has gone red. The sounds of explosions are already chasing them. A blast of dust brushes the backs of her legs, which, she notices, are no longer moving. Lot tells her to run. He tells her not to look back, but all she can think about is back. Everything she knows is back. Everything she loves is back. The only place she wants to be is back.

QUIET HOURS
Lilly Dancyger

The room was so dark that even though I'd been lying in bed with my eyes open for at least an hour, I couldn't see anything. A thick darkness. There were no windows on my side of the studio, and the one window on the other side looked out into a brick wall—at least it did during the day. Now it just looked out into more darkness. There was only the sound of rain against that window, sounding so active and alive it made me jealous.

Finally, I decided that trying to sleep was pointless. I climbed down from my loft bed and felt around, finding the clothes I'd worn earlier by texture. My eyes were wide open, straining, but I did it all by feel: the thick, heavy jeans; the scratchy wool sweater; the already-wet-from-earlier boots. I pulled them all on slowly, and carefully walked toward the door with my fingertips running along the wall to guide me. I opened the door as little as possible so as to not let in enough light to wake my mother. The tiny apartment we shared in a tenement building on the Lower East Side was a true studio—all one room. The fold-out couch that doubled as her bed was on one side, by the window, and my loft bed next to the fridge and stove was on the other side, with about twenty feet between them. The lack of privacy was hard to deal with as a fifteen-year-old insomniac. Once my mother was asleep, I couldn't make any noise or turn on a light. Even the soft clicking of the keyboard if I tried to sit in the dark and talk to my friends on AIM would wake her up. So my options were to lie still in the darkness for hours, or sneak out into the night.

I stood at the top of the stairs with my eyes closed for almost a minute, overwhelmed by the bright fluorescent lights in the hallway. Once I'd adjusted to the light, I ran down the stairs, excited to be free, moving, like the rain. I hesitated for just a moment at the downstairs door; I hadn't even thought to bring an umbrella. Oh well. I ducked into the rain. For the first block, I walked quickly with my head down and shoulders up, as if I could shield myself from the steady, soft rain that was hitting my face and plastering my hair onto my head and neck. But once I'd been thoroughly soaked by the downpour, my steps became slow and purposeful, and I looked up at the streetlights, letting the rain run over my face and wash away my nerves.

Sometimes on these late-night walks I'd pick a stoop to sit on, chain smoking and scribbling in my notebook. Other nights I would just walk aimlessly for hours and hours, observing the city, narrating stories in my head. Walking in zigzags across lower Manhattan, singing softly to myself, "I'm not sleepy and there is no place I'm going to." Walking across the Williamsburg Bridge at dawn, to watch the sun rise over the water, and writing frantic poetry. Amused by the delirious state I would reach after a night of wandering, I decided to take a sort of satisfaction in the restlessness that I sometimes thought was just part of being young, and sometimes worried was a critical defect in my wiring. I thought

I would find what I was looking for on the streets at night, even though I didn't know what that was. I often imagined my moment of epiphany, could almost feel the feeling of "Yes, that's it!" but the image in my mind was always too blurry and fragmented to see what it was that I'd realized—like losing your page in a book right as you're approaching the climax of the story.

I learned the patterns of the waves of people I would pass at different times of night: usually by the time I escaped onto the street, I would emerge into the end of the night for the nightlife crowd, women dressed up in heels and short skirts, bros yelling way louder than necessary about whether or not to go to one more bar, all walking in groups or pairs, stumbling and laughing. A loud, sloppy energy in sharp contrast with the dark quiet I'd just left, but that I welcomed even as I avoided swerving drunks.

Then there was a lull, about an hour between four and five when there was almost no one left on the streets and I could walk for blocks and blocks, even on the busiest avenues of the East Village, and the only people I would pass were those who slept on flattened cardboard boxes and under tattered blankets as I slowed my steps to avoid waking them. It felt like everyone in the city but me was asleep. This was my favorite time of day; the hour I would wait for, that I felt like I was walking toward, when it felt like I had the whole city to myself: the quiet and space, the streets there just for me to pace and pace until I found whatever it was they had to show me. I felt endless then.

That night in the rain, I hadn't looked at the clock before sneaking out. I imagined it couldn't be later than two or three, but the streets were already empty, cleared early by the steady pelting rain. It was a warm early autumn night, so even though I was soaking wet and my socks made a deep squelch with every step, I wasn't cold. When my sweater became heavy with water I tied it around my waist and let the rain run over my bare arms and flatten my curly hair against my shoulder blades.

During the day, I was surly, an angry teenager with disappointment and nameless need burning under my skin and pounding in my ears. I dropped out of high school, I fought with my mother, our screams bouncing off the walls in our tiny apartment. I tried to drown my restlessness in cheap vodka, to smoke it out with unfiltered cigarettes, to escape it with hallucinogens that sometimes worked for a few hours until they wore off. But the water was cool and soft and the sounds of the rain muffled everything else swirling around in my mind: the steady patter on the street mixed with louder drumming on taut awnings, echoing drips from scaffolding, and the rush of small streams forming in gutters. The traffic lights directing empty streets threw green and red splashes on the wet asphalt, transforming avenues into noir stills. Once in a while, a delivery truck or a lone taxi with its lights on would drive past, parting the water on the street like a shark's fin, but mostly I saw no one. The particular buzzing calm of catching a place that's usually bustling with people in a quiet moment is not the same as somewhere that's always empty. It's more like an exhale, an in-between moment where anything is possible. I walked for hours, slowly, then hopped the fence and sat on my favorite bench in

Tompkins, eyes closed and face pointed up toward the sky, the rain never letting up. It felt like standing at the edge of the ocean.

Just before dawn, that window of time where the sky isn't getting lighter yet but you can feel that it wants to, the rain slowed to a drizzle. After hours of the cacophony of heavy rain, the new quiet plus the anticipation of almost-dawn created a buzz in the air that made my head swim; every tiny sound amplified. When the sky finally did start to get lighter in the slightest increments of gray, I wasn't sure at first whether it was really happening or if it was just my heightened senses; the fog washed out of my brain. But then I saw the first groggy people trickling onto the streets and knew the day was on its way.

Always right around five, the first wave of early-morning commuters would appear like the first flowers to bloom through snow. Bakers and cooks and janitors, the hardest workers in the city, freshly showered and tired-eyed, walking quickly, stirring the previously still air. I always felt reinvigorated by this wave; filled with a rush of astonishment at how many people worked tirelessly every day to keep this city running. I wondered if they'd gotten enough sleep the night before; if they'd snuck out of their own apartments in the dark, like I had, careful not to wake sleeping spouses or children.

I nodded good morning to these people on their way to work, genuinely hoping each one would have a good day. Some smiled back and some gave me a curious look, probably wondering why I was so soaked when it was barely raining. At this point in the pre-morning, I set out toward a specific destination for the first time on this long walk: toward home. Sometimes, even going in circles, I might have ended up miles from home, and would have to make my way slowly back.

Around six, the next wave of people started as a trickle; the women with blowouts, trench coats, and big sunglasses, protecting their perfectly styled hair from the light mist with umbrellas, hailing cabs with hands holding venti coffees; the men in suits talking loudly into their cell phones, startling me with the first voices I'd heard in hours. First just the most industrious few, then more, and more, the density of people on the street increasing steadily in time with the brightening of the sun as it started to cut through the clouds, in a crescendo of the new day. It felt like I'd lived through a year of seasons in just a few hours, the dark and wet being burned away by brightness and activity.

As soon as the sun was above the horizon and the streets were fully populated, I would sneak back into the apartment and my bed, so that when my mother woke up it would look like I'd been sleeping peacefully all night. I never knew whether she'd be angry, or worried, or curious, if she knew that I spent so many nights walking alone through empty streets, but I didn't feel like finding out. Instead, I tiptoed in as quietly as I'd left, closing the door behind me so, very, slowly. I stripped off the wet clothes and draped them over the back of the chair under my loft bed, exactly where they'd been the night before, and climbed slowly into bed. Lying there, my hair soaking my pillow, my heart racing with the sudden stillness of my body after a night of pacing, I felt utterly exhausted, my limbs heavy and buzzing. And finally, I could sleep.

II

THE CHASE
K.C. Mead-Brewer

Here it is, The Fool, stepping off his cliff. *I love you*,
he says, I'm saying, and fuck. Thank god the road
is there to save me from myself. It's always known
how to love me best, by being there, by running away
from me. Every mile I gain on it, it's got thousands more
in every direction. My previous lives have all felt its
pull and stretch, the tease of its bending smile: when I
was Jonah boarding the ship, out out! to the sea!, crisp
salt air filling my chest with hope even as a hungry
god lurked in the waters beneath; the road, the road.
When I was Persephone climbing aboard my lover's
oil-black motorcycle—the way his engine rumbled, it
sounded like the growling of a three-headed dog. When
I was Merlin deliciously insane on the dirt paths of
ancient England, my youth rushing toward my creaking
body even as the wilderness tangled in on my mind,
tempting me toward kings and lakes and crystal caves.
When I was Odysseus and everything, everywhere, a
wine-dark sea. When I was all one hundred and one
of those Dalmatians sneaking off into the dark, fresh
mud squelching beneath my paws, my fur coat the night
sky's wild inversion. When I was with Allen and Jack
and taking their poetry like medicine against all that
my preacher-father taught me in our years running

through every parish in North Carolina. When I was the hurricane that dragged my mother's house out to sea and everything started again. How it's always been a dawn in my chest. A notion clear and untouchable as light. My soul bending toward the scent of circuses—popcorn, elephants, funnel cake; the chalky taste of that sad clown's makeup as we licked each other—and the blaring of foghorns, the crunch of waves against a ship's hull, the violent romance of a pirate's laugh as they take you in their arms and swagger, "Kiss me if you want to live." My grandmother, several greats back, smeared her naked body with blood jelly in hopes of drifting up to her lover, the moon. She scrawled with the black ink from a snake's fang into a diary that now bakes in my old Impala's glove compartment: *Only ye who wish to be chased shall run away*, and yes, Grandmother, yes! If you don't chase me, how will I know you love me? If you don't chase me, how will you ever taste my dust? If you don't chase me, whose arms will I fall into at the edge of the world? What is a great fuck but a great running away—a flight into another's body, another's pleasure, another's breath. I don't care about sex, but I care about this: the road. The motion. The glorious roar of the horizon, a cheek so soft, so exquisitely curved, you'll reach to touch it again and again and helplessly again. If you aren't running by now, you're either dead or much braver than me. If you aren't running by now, there's nothing I can do for you. If you aren't running by now, sweetheart, it's because you've already been caught.

CIRCLING BACK

Matt Cantor

Mr. White paid two thousand dollars to name a pair of stars, a thousand apiece, and he paid two billion dollars for a spaceship half the size of a living room.

People will tell you that spaceships cost a lot to buy because of the amazing things they can do, zipping here to there faster than light—a dozen times faster, a thousand times faster, isn't that amazing? But Mr. White, he knows better, so he knows that spaceships cost a lot to buy because of how much they cost to make, and because of how much people are willing to pay for them on top of that. Mr. White was willing to pay a lot on top for this one.

He would have paid a lot more to name those stars, too. He would have paid everything for those. Those were gargantuan stars, both larger than fifty suns. Those two stars in Andromeda that Mr. White had paid to name, their light first hit Earth two million years before he was born, and they'd be burning in the telescopes of Earth two million years after he was gone. That's what he'd been rightly promised, and for all of those two million years they'd be called exactly what he'd paid a thousand dollars apiece to call them. Mr. White is a man who knows a deal when he sees one.

After his first day in space, he's traveled two light years. If his spaceship had the right sort of receiver, he could pick up a very grainy signal of the very first bits of news coverage of the Shelf Collapse, a hundred different islands suddenly gobbled up by the sea—only just the shortest blip of it at how fast he's going, but if he came to a stop and if his ship had the right sort of receiver, he could watch the news.

But of course Mr. White doesn't quite understand this, and his ship doesn't have the right sort of receiver. If his ship's telescope was strong enough, and if he knew just the right place to park, Mr. White could skip the coverage and watch the actual thing happen. But of course Mr. White doesn't quite understand this, either, and his ship's telescope isn't strong enough, and he wouldn't bother anyways. What could he learn that he doesn't already know? Things happened like they always happened, like they're always happening, very quickly, all at once, much too fast to see them coming, and there's no going back. When Mr. White was a child, trucks all had wheels, and now trucks don't need wheels anymore, and now Mr. White is hurtling through space faster than anything else in the universe. There's only so much that can fit into a lifetime, and there's too much trying to fit into Mr. White's lifetime. When Mr. White was a child, all the new cars had special driver warning systems and auto-braking front cameras. Everything should have been even safer after that. Mr. White has too much already cramming into his lifetime for him to be able to make sense of it.

After two days, he's six light years out from Earth— six light years in two days, that's fast, but he's still getting faster every second; he's got a long way to go. Mr. White's day goes round and round. He wakes up in his bed, at the back end of the ship's little cabin, and he moves clockwise from there to the tiny bathroom, where he uses the toilet, brushes his teeth, takes a shower. Then he gets dressed and goes clockwise to the pilot's seat to make sure that the ship is still on course, which it is, obviously, the computer is making sure of that. It's the computer's job to make sure that Mr. White's ship ends up in the exact spot where those two stars are, and computers are very good at those sorts of jobs. But Mr. White checks all the same because he knows better than to just blindly trust.

After checking, Mr. White goes clockwise to the kitchenette to make himself some toast. That's the most he can make for himself from scratch; it was always his husband who'd done the cooking. He goes clockwise again to sit on his bed as he eats. The pilot's seat would be just as good, but he'd have to go counterclockwise to get back there, and that's not really the way he's been going. Mr. White eats breakfast in bed, and then he goes clockwise again, uses the toilet again, and then he goes clockwise one more time and he sits in the pilot's seat for a few hours, watching the universe go by until lunch.

Ten light years total by dinner. If his ship's telescope was strong enough, and if he knew just the right place to park, Mr. White could sit and watch the crosswalk at the corner of Janvers Road and Heathley Street in Yellowbluff, Michigan, and every lingering question he's ever had could be answered. No more gaps. No incident logs, no dashcams or testimony, nothing to piece together.

Round and round. Faster and faster.

After six days, Mr. White's ship is about eight hundred light years from Earth. If he had a strong enough telescope, which he doesn't, and if he understood these things, which he doesn't, he could glance back at Earth and watch the crusades from above. He could watch them all fight, and he would know that if anyone asked any of the soldiers on either side why they were fighting, they would probably say something or other about being watched from above by someone with power beyond all their comprehension, and maybe Mr. White would have seen some deep beauty in that, or maybe he would have just found it funny.

At eight days, Mr. White's ship is far enough for him to look back and see Christ, and at lunchtime he gets up from the pilot's seat and goes clockwise to the kitchenette for some mashed potatoes. That's the other thing he can make for himself all right, mashed potatoes. Twelve years of mashed potatoes and toast in Molly's lunches, or at least when it wasn't Justin's turn. He goes clockwise, eats on his bed, he goes clockwise again, uses the toilet again—round and round, the water swirls round and round—clockwise, back to the pilot's seat.

Christ lived for thirty years before things really started happening with him. Christ was a carpenter mostly until he was thirty and then things started happening very quickly, all at once, much too fast to see it coming, and there was no going back. Mr. White doesn't believe in Christ, not really, but he knows that things are always happening that way; that part he believes.

Faster and faster. When eighteen days have passed, the ship is a full hundred thousand light years from Earth. But a hundred thousand light years from Earth is nothing. Mr. White's stars are in a place so far from Earth that when he gets there and looks back, if he has a strong enough telescope, he'll be able to see humans developing the very first stone tools—two and a half-million light years, that's how long ago he'll have to travel to reach the spot where his stars are.

Two and a half-million light years is maybe nothing, too; you'd have to go a lot further than that if you wanted to look back and see dinosaurs.

A hundred thousand light years is enough for the ship to be out of the Milky Way, at least. Right before dinner, for the very first time in this whole trip, Mr. White points the ship's telescope backwards to get a look at his galaxy, which is spinning rather quickly in the wrong direction.

Lots and lots of strange things happen when you start getting close to the speed of light, and Mr. White doesn't really know about any of them—and he really doesn't have to because none of those strange things happen when you're going faster. Going faster than light is a very different sort of game, none of that relativity mess comes into play, bending and stretching and slowing and junk. When you're going faster, the time of the universe moves as fast as you're going, backwards behind you, forwards in front of you, and it all makes good sense actually if you sit down with a pen and paper and try to work it out. Behind Mr. White, time runs backwards at thousands of years per second because every second he's racing thousands of light years away, towards Andromeda, which is spinning too, the right way round—faster and faster, faster and faster, round and round and round.

Mr. White doesn't watch the Milky Way for more than a moment or so before glancing away. He doesn't like the way it's turning.

He goes clockwise to the kitchenette. Prepacked grilled cheese sandwich with mayo and pickles. Mr.

White goes clockwise, he eats on his bed, and then he goes clockwise to the bathroom, uses the toilet one last time, brushes his teeth—and then he goes clockwise to the pilot's seat to make sure the ship is still on course. He doesn't want to just leave it to the computer. He goes clockwise to the kitchenette, and clockwise again back to his bed instead of simply walking straight across the cabin because that's just the way he's been going—round and round.

The whole night, he's dreaming about wheels. Trucks don't even have wheels, but he remembers it that way. He hadn't been there himself, so his brain has helpfully done the work of piecing together a memory of it for him because his brain is just a computer, isn't it?—and computers aren't very good at not doing things like that. His brain has given the truck wheels because all the trucks Mr. White ever saw as a child, they all had wheels. There's only so much you can handle in a lifetime, and Mr. White has handled much too much.

He dreams of wheels and screeching tires, but of course there were no tires, no screeching. He dreams of screaming. He dreams of his ship going off course while he's asleep. He dreams of everything being all right for a while and then it happens very quickly, all at once, much too fast to see it coming, and there's no going back—his ship swerves off course and by the time he wakes up, who knows where he'll be? Mr. White is hopelessly lost and he doesn't know it. The ship's computer is piloting him towards the exact spot he wants to go, the exact location of those two stars he paid to name, and he'll reach that spot soon, no question about it; computers are very good at those sorts of jobs. The math is simple and the path is straight. But Mr. White is hopelessly lost and he doesn't know it and the computer doesn't know it because it's not that sort of math.

Round and round go the days, round and round.

At a million light years or so, give-take, Mr. White points the ship's telescope at Andromeda. He finds his stars, orbiting each other, and he can't for the life of him tell them apart. Fifty thousand light years per second means fifty thousand years per second; with an orbital period of just twelve years, the stars are whirling around each other much too fast, much too fast to look like anything other than a halo. From Earth, they'd seemed entirely motionless—static, eternal. For two million years after he's gone, Mr. White's stars will burn in the telescopes of Earth, barely moving. Two million years for two thousand American dollars. Mr. White knows a deal when he sees one.

Or maybe not. He finally lets himself laugh at something, just a little bit, because supply and demand are such funny things; in a fifteen-billion-year-old universe, a million years here or there is practically worthless.

He knows that the universe is fifteen billion years old, roughly, but he doesn't know how he knows it—he doesn't know how anyone could know a thing like that, and he doesn't care enough to try and find out. He's willing to take that one on faith. We know the universe is fifteen billion years old because that's how far away we can see—fifteen billion light years ago, those are the earliest things we can see, and Mr. White is hopelessly lost.

The next time he wakes up, his ship has come to a complete stop. Here he is, right where he wanted it to take him. He doesn't know that yet when he wakes up; he has to go clockwise to the bathroom first, use the

toilet, brush his teeth, take a shower, and then he has
to go clockwise again to check that the ship is still on
course, and only then does he see what's happened, and
when he sees what's happened, he's absolutely certain
that there must have been some mistake.

There must have been.

There is nothing but dust and gas where Mr. White's
stars should be, but the computer is assuring him that
there's been no mistake.

Two people crossing the street, four people on the
sidewalk, simple math—there had never been a mistake.
A cousin already came to identify the remains, no mistake.

This is the place.

Mr. White doesn't eat breakfast or lunch or dinner,
and he doesn't go to bed. For nearly thirty hours, he
just stares.

When he finally does eat, it's barely a bite, and he
doesn't do it on his bed—no momentum. He sits in the
pilot's seat and he reads through the scientific encyclopedia helpfully included with the ship's computer. He
reads about time and space and stars. He learns how
we know that the universe is fifteen billion years old.
He learns that if he had a strong enough telescope and
knew the right spot to park, he could look back on Earth
and watch himself be born—not really, because he was
born indoors, like most people, but the writers of the
encyclopedia thought it was cute to include anyways.
He learns that he could pick any moment and watch it
happen—forwards or backwards, as many times as he
liked, if he had a strong enough telescope and knew the
right spot to park.

He tells the ship's computer to turn around and jump
a hundred thousand light years back towards the Milky

Way, and it does, and a few days later, there he is. But there are no stars through the telescope, not in the spot he needs them to be. Another hundred thousand light years before that, another hundred thousand years further away, still no luck. He jumps fifty thousand, and there they are. Mr. White keeps track of all this on a piece of paper—several pieces of paper. He could just log it all in the computer, but that's not really the feeling of the thing. He jumps forward. He jumps backward. Smaller and smaller leaps every time, shorter and shorter times every leap—he's zeroing in on the moment. The stars are there. Then they're not. Then they are. Then they are again. Then they're not again. Then they are again.

"Thirty-five light hours forwards," he tells the computer, and twenty minutes later the stars are gone. "Sixteen light hours backwards"—and there they are. "Fourteen forwards."—gone. "Four backwards."—still gone. "Again."—there they are.

And he's found it. It's happening.

It is a common misconception that stars explode in an instant—it's an easy thing to get wrong, and it's easy to see why. They're such violent things, how could the explosion be anything but instantaneous?—a wink of light, brief and blinding, and then nothing. There is some truth to that; compared to the life of a star, death is a heartbeat. These stars' light reached Earth two million years before Mr. White was born, and they'll burn in Earth's telescopes for two million years after he's gone, and next to four million years, nearly everything passes in a heartbeat—very quick, all at once, much too fast to see coming, and there's no going back.

It all depends on who you ask. A truck comes barreling down the road and the brakes fail and there are two people crossing the street and there are four people on the sidewalk and sure there's a tree to steer into but the pallet of cell phones in the back cost six people's lives to make and the computer calculates that consumers will be willing to pay an extra eight hundred thousand dollars on top of that so the math is simple and the path is straight and the supernova is so violent that both stars are blasted to smithereens—but only those two. We all know a deal when we see one.

Minutes pass. Half an hour, and still the distant light carries on, steady, cold. On and on and on. Two hours, three hours, the light carries on—by now, though, it's properly over, this is just a rotting sort of glow. AG-1718A-Justin and AG 1718B-Molly are dead, mangled, and how could a cousin identify their corpses from the gas and the dust?—but there's been no mistake. The light carries on and the truck carries on after the crosswalk, right on towards the depot, carefully compensating the rest of the way for its failed brakes, the math is simple, there's been no mistake, what's to stop for?

"Again," says Mr. White, and the computer jumps him again back another four light hours; its whole decision plays in reverse—everything comes racing inwards from the edges of the screen, coalescing into a pair of stars, and then Mr. White watches them die again. "Again," he says.

He watches them die again.

"Again."

And again.

"Again."

And again.

It's exactly like he remembers.

SELF-CARE

Sarah Tollok

I t has come to our attention here at *Treat Yourself Magazine* that some of the self-care tips offered in last month's issue were misinterpreted by readers. Our legal team has advised us to offer clarification around several of these. This is in no way an admission of responsibility for any such actions that our readers may have taken prior to or subsequent to this clarification being offered.

DO: Unclench your jaw. Sometimes during prolonged, focused tasks, one can fall into clenching one's jaw. Set a timer for ten- to thirty-minute intervals to check if you are retaining tension in your jaw or even your brow as you work. Consciously relax those facial muscles and maybe even give a brief self-massage.

DO NOT: Unhinge your jaw so far, so very far, that out pours all of the alternative selves that you usually keep tucked in your throat, tangled in the chords of voices that never reach the wind. These selves, if allowed to tumble out like so many clowns from a comically compact beige car, could run amuck. They could quit your job, buy a boat, start a YouTube channel, cure cancer, clean the ocean, try shrooms, fuck your neighbor, fuck your neighbor's wife, get a face tattoo, start a community garden, invent an engine that will safely carry the human race to other planets once we have used up Earth, push the unassuming gray button which launches the bombs that trigger a nuclear winter, or they could even write something that inspires an entire generation to throw off the shackles of gendered expectations.

DO: Hydrate! Drink at least two liters of water a day. Always have a water bottle within arm's reach to make this as easy as possible. Try a squeeze of citrus, infusing some cut fruit, or even throwing in some torn mint leaves to make things more interesting and colorful.

DO NOT: Drink so much water that your body becomes entirely diluted, your skin floats away, your cells burst and unravel, and you become part of the planet's water cycle. You will then exist as the tears of your children, the piss of the feral cat that wanders through your yard at night, the morning dew on the grass of the playground down the street, the puddle that someone intentionally drives through to splash the homeless woman, the spit drunkenly exchanged in a kiss between two people who don't know each other's last names, and the droplet that slowly wells on the edge of the cut tulip stem.

DO: Get out in nature! Did you know that breathing in the essential oils naturally released into the air by trees can significantly decrease your cortisol levels? Emerging studies have found that test subjects with chronic conditions, such as diabetes and nerve-related pain, who spend thirty minutes a week outside among trees use less medication to manage their symptoms than those in a control group that spend that same amount of time relaxing in an indoor setting.

DO NOT: Walk out into the woods, be they the deep woods or those in your local patch between suburban development borders, strip naked, lie down, sink your fingers into the soft soil, wriggle and writhe into the debris of the forest floor, then lie so still for so long that you start making contact with the mycorrhizal network of fungi that runs between the trees. Do not become part of the network, sharing your water, nitrogen, and carbon with the redbuds, oak, and pine trees. Do not lose yourself in the chemical and electrical whispers of danger from chainsaws, chippers, and drought, denying to yourself and your new brethren that you are more like the shortsighted man with his hand on the trigger than you are with your sisters who reach for the sky.

DO: Remember to breathe. Especially when anxious thoughts start playing on repeat, close your eyes and take three truly deep cleansing breaths. Inhaling for a count of seven, retaining your breath for a count of five, then exhale slowly for a count of seven or until you have completely emptied out the breath.

DO NOT: Breathe in so deeply and completely that you soon contain everything that is and ever was, holding it in within yourself. Please note, there will no longer be a "you" because self is defined in relation to "other." Since the whole of time and space is now contained within "you," there is nothing to reference "yourself" against.

Remembering to count at this point will not be effective because, again, time no longer exists and numbers/quantities will be moot. Then, if "you" do finally breath out again, realize that existence will not just start back up as it was, but will rather be rebirthed in a manner that is entirely newly organized. All that inhabit it will not remember the old version and will carry on as if it always was the way it now is. They would be right insofar as you and your unspeakably deep breath are both the destroyer and the mother of realities.

DO: Get moving! Even just a brisk five-minute walk around the block or up a few flights of stairs can get your endorphins flowing.

DO NOT: Move, then move faster, then exponentially faster. Do not creep closer and closer to the speed of light. Do not become perpetual acceleration. Do not move so fast that the world ahead of you looms in fast/slow violet, and, when you glance back over your shoulder, you see where you have been, bathed in shades of crimson.

SANDWICHED

DW McKinney

The bread bag rustles as my palm skims over the loaf's heel. Usually the heels are unloved, but the taste and quality of the buttermilk loaf mean that we will likely eat the heel instead of tossing it into the garbage. I grab two slices, and the bread squishes under my fingertips. That's a good sign. It means the dry desert air has not yet rendered them stale. It means more of the sandwich will get eaten this time. It means one less slight, one less comment to deter my transition into the adjacent universe.

I take the slices from the bag and sniff them; they smell good. I flip them around to check for mold, an extra precaution. It's a habit I developed once I had children and sickness became an ever-present disruption. I prefer peace anyway I can get it. There is never enough of it, never enough to scrape out between working and mothering, between being a wife and the day-to-day minutia that comes with living.

I close the bread bag, spinning it around to coil the plastic into a tight rope before sealing it with the ragged twist tie. The spinning pulls in the kitchen and it winds with the bag, blurring the edges and exposing the tears between the universes I straddle.

Laughter rises in the back of my mind. Wood crackles

and sparks. Flames burst into the forefront, blocking out the image of my youngest daughter, who is sitting cross-legged on the living room carpet watching television. I walk toward the laughter, toward men waiting near a roaring bonfire.

Is my sandwich ready yet, my youngest asks from the living room. Her gaze is fixed on the cartoons in front of her. I tell her I just started, to be patient. She'll get what she wants soon enough. I could make the sandwich faster, but rushing has become a hallmark of my life with children. I am always rushing awake, rushing around the house, rushing out the door. All this rushing to satisfy other people as quickly as possible while I'm often left with crumbs. So, I take it slow when I can. I indulge the cinematic sweetness that seeps from in between the mundanity of everyday living. This is how I escape. This is how I keep myself satisfied.

I toss the slices onto the plastic plate waiting on the counter. My maternal grandmother was the only one who made pb and j's for me. I would eat the sandwiches on a tin tea tray while I watched *Scooby-Doo, Where Are You!*, wishing I could solve mysteries. Wishing I was someplace where magic was more attainable. I've attained that magic now.

My vision slides to the left and I reach the bonfire. Anticipation gives way to hunger at my arrival. One of the men smiles down at me. His black hair is oiled and curls past his shoulders. A sharp-toothed grin parts his thick beard as he extends an aluminum can toward me. In the here and now, I walk toward the cabinet. My hands reach out. I hold a full can of beer. I hold a half-empty jar of peanut butter.

I move back to the counter, but I remain at the bonfire. A butter knife glints in my hand. For a moment, my mind stutters. *What is the knife for?* I ask in dual voices. I disappear from the fire, from the sound of bodies shifting, from wolves gathering, to pull myself fully into the present. I need the knife to spread the peanut butter. But I also need jelly.

The refrigerator door opens with a suctioned pop. I retrieve the Bonne Maman raspberry preserves from the door's bottom shelf. My youngest asks me again if her sandwich is ready. It's not. Guilt burns the back of my throat. I am not neglectful, but I am constantly wrestling between feeling capable of doing so much more than my physical body allows and willfully fleeing into a world where I live my fullest potential. Where I am more in control, so powerful beyond measure that I would never dream of making a simple sandwich.

A thick nutty aroma fills my nose as I unscrew the Jif. The peanut butter is curled up inside the jar. It reminds me of a dune. Sands shift in a world far away, where a full moon punctuates the flat velvet sky. Growls rumble behind me—

—I cuss and disrupt the dune with the knife. The faster I finish the sandwich, the faster I can leave the kitchen to hunt. I slap a scoop of peanut butter across the bread and smear it back and forth until it's even. Reaching across the counter, I pull a napkin from the stack that came with yesterday's takeout. Wiping the knife clean, I fold the napkin into a square and lay the knife on top of it.

My youngest looks up at me and we smile at each other. *Almost done, sweet pea*, I say. I'm aware that it may be taking too long. That this the longest it's ever taken me to make a sandwich because I indulged myself one too many times in the process. The preserves pop open with a metallic click, releasing a sweet fruit scent. I scoop out a lump with the knife and smear it over the bread. The raspberries remind me of cheap gore in a horror movie. I take it in my mind's eye and fashion it between the snarling maw of wolves—my pack—tearing into an animal's hide. I'm so close, tugging my focus to their imagined direction. I want to leave so badly, I would flee out the back door if it led to a chilly, moonlit forest. It almost feels like I could get away with just a peek. But I don't.

Carefully, I place the two slices together so that they match up, letting none of the preserves bleed out. I raise the knife. The sandwich divides cleanly in two. I cut the sandwich again, dividing the two long rectangles into four neat squares. No need to cut the crusts off. Sometimes my daughter eats them. Sometimes she doesn't. It's likely she will gobble them up the fresher the bread is.

I grab the plate and inhale as I place it in front of my daughter. She looks away from the television long enough to peel open the tiny sandwiches. I wonder when her imagination will widen like a gulf and if she'll have to sift through the burden of maladaptive daydreaming like me. She smiles at me, then shreds the tiny sandwiches with her teeth. For a moment, I see the flash of many razor-sharp teeth gnashing and tearing away at their prey, then it's just my daughter with a lump of preserves in the corner of her mouth.

I clean the counter, then slip away, grinning wide as howling fills my ears.

Peanut Butter and Jelly Sandwich

Ingredients:
2 slices of buttermilk bread

1–1½ tablespoons of Jif creamy peanut butter

1 tablespoon of Bonne Maman raspberry preserves

A dash of wild daydreams

Directions:
1. Place a plate on a flat surface, then drift toward the welcoming bonfire.

2. Take two slices of bread and place them side by side on the plate. Spread peanut butter on one slice of bread. Transform into your second self. Spread the preserves on the second slice of bread.

3. Combine the slices together with the peanut butter and preserves in the middle.

4. Lay the sandwich flat on the plate and cut the sandwich into triangles, rectangles, squares, or eat whole. Listen to the beckoning calls of your pack.

CORPSE MOM DISCOVERS THE TEN-STEP KOREAN SKIN CARE ROUTINE

Hema Nataraju

C orpse Mom has discovered the best thing in life after her death. With her new evening ritual—the ten-step Korean skin care routine, she's entered a delightful new universe. How lovely it is to be dead, she thinks, to not have to worry about school nights, prepping lunchboxes, answering work emails, or having "married-for-donkey's-years" sex with her husband.

Something's been rattling in her chest since yesterday, though—a worry, a seed of anxiety. It's killing her ritual and her mood.

She puts it aside for later and starts with the first step, the double cleanse. The cleansing balm is creamy at first, it becomes an oil when it touches her skin, and when she emulsifies it with water, it transforms into a milky liquid! She marvels at its shape-shifting ability and then she marvels at her marveling. When was the last time she had marveled at something?

The worry rankles in her chest again. It's louder now. There isn't much skin on her ribs to muffle its sound. Something happened at yesterday's graveyard group counseling session. But what?

She washes her face with a gentle foaming cleanser. It has no smell, so it doesn't bring up any memories. Just the way Corpse Mom likes it. Next is the AHA/BHA toner. She sprays a few pumps onto her palm and pat, pat, pats it on her face, around the hollows that used to be her eyes. Her skin is so taut, so clear, like glass, she can see her defined jawline right through her papery skin. No acne scars. Her skin has shed its memories of adult acne and low self-esteem she's suffered from all her life. She turns her face to the left and then to the right and admires herself in the small mirror piece she found two plots away in the graveyard.

Then she remembers. It was something at the graveyard counseling session. Paul from two plots away missed his kids so much, he tried to escape the graveyard. The higher-ups had zapped him. It was safe to say they would never see Paul again. Shocked OMGs and some crying from the group followed. Everyone could see why Paul did what he did. They have all thought of running back to their families at some point.

Only Corpse Mom remained silent throughout the session.

She can never remember what comes next. A serum, ampoule, essence? Does the collagen mask come before or after moisturizer? She remembers that she used to remember everything when she was alive—her kids' schedules, doctor appointments, work stuff, her husband's travel schedule, play dates, grocery refills, everything, but now she cannot even remember her husband's name or their kids' faces.

The graveyard counselor had said trying to escape the graveyard was futile, but why hasn't she even tried? Was she a terrible mom? Is she a terrible mom?

She sits on her gravestone in the thick moonless darkness. Her little apothecary of bottles with droppers and sprays and dark-colored tubs are gathered around her, ready to give her their everything. Her back faces the epitaph—Beloved Mom, Wife, Daughter. Who Gave Everything to Family. Forever in Our Hearts.

She rubs a few drops of green tea serum between her palms and presses it onto her skin. Her skin laps it up, but she tries, tries, tries not to feel joy, not to focus on glass skin. She closes her eyes and summons every brain cell to help her remember her family's faces, tries to want to run away, tries to be a good mom again.

TO THE MAN AT THE PUMP NEXT TO ME AT THE BP IN MARBLE HILL ON THE NIGHT OF MY HUSBAND'S BIRTHDAY AFTER I'VE KICKED MY FAMILY OUT OF AN ALMOST MOVING CAR

Emily James

I came for you because I knew this green-lit station was the only place I could be saved. On my way down I pushed the pedal harder and didn't apologize, even when the city bus tried to turn, needed me to brake and put it in reverse, back up so it could clear the intersection. The driver eyed me and I eyed them back, not today not today and we almost crashed and I didn't care because guess what we fucking made it work. I kept going past the flowers in a plastic cup by the stop sign where a woman was run over months back, when the air was colder, she was out alone walking, maybe running away, maybe on her way to you too. Down the hill to fill the tank is the furthest place I can think of other than a hotel in Westchester or Upstate New York or

Canada or fucking Iceland, and still I consider it, going to any of those places, even though I only have this one outfit on, these jeans and this cute crop top sweater with bell sleeves I got off Craigslist, perfect for a night like tonight, a night I didn't realize would end in me meeting you, a birthday celebration for my husband with my two daughters—the ones with honey-colored eyes who'd be sure to splash sparkles on their eyelids before we left, a little on their cheeks even, and I'm supposed to be their mommy and keep my calm and cool even after I struggle to get them to stop whining through the hibachi dinner, the juice too sour, the rice too sticky, the flames too high, as I sat there in my new-used sweater that made me feel cute just hours ago in front of a mirror, trying to pretend I can mother and live at the same time. On the way home when they started to scream because we'd turned the music too loud, swaying our shoulders as husband and wife, trying to feel the beat inside ourselves and become who we know we were when we met and rode bikes all night along the East River, lay next to the litter beneath the trees covered in our sweat and squeezed each other's hands, "it's too loud," covering their little ears and we ignore them because for just one fucking second we want to feel something that belongs to us but they won't stop, their squeals louder than the radio bass and I look back and realize I'm not cut out for this, this sweater that bares my stomach, these ripped boyfriend jeans, this role of just shaving off pieces of myself all day long layer by layer for the girls I need the most, this is what made me kick them all out of the car outside the apartment building and scream for them to leave, LEAVE leave and tell the youngest to watch her hands in the car door as she sobbed—where's Mommy going? I was on my way to you, a stranger, bathing in silence after the door slammed and the quiet of the night sky, the leather of the seats, the trip around the wide-turning bus, I didn't yet know you were waiting for me at the station, the $4.19 per gallon and my account damn close near to zero from that expensive dinner with the soy sauce in squirty bottles and the twisty straws, blasting my music now in peace. Standing next to the pump I stick in a card and bang on the regular unleaded button, it can take a hit, my belly in the cool air for you to see, I smile at you and you smile back and I think about stopping at a store to pick up some contact solution so I can sleep at the hotel, I have underwear on and how good those heavy white blankets would feel over my shirtless body, rubbing over my tits, a TV on low all through the night and a big window that won't open with its dusty blinds, I'm so sorry because even though right now I love you without even saying hello, I wouldn't even bring you, I'd go alone, the numbers rise, ten dollars, twenty dollars, and when you stare back at me you don't cry, thirty dollars, forty dollars, I hold the lever with the grease on the side of my palm and listen to the glug glug with your gaze the perfect weight that lets me stand. You wouldn't dare ask me for shit tonight. You wouldn't expect a goddamn thing except for maybe my pussy to be wet like this gasoline as it glug glug glugs into the tank, the bass of the music still shaking my car windows. It's just the two of us under these bright lights we can't look directly into, fifty dollars, sixty dollars, and maybe I'll buy a lotto ticket, maybe I'll buy a Gatorade, maybe some ice in a bag or a toothbrush for my life with those dusty curtains and the long rod that pulls them open and closed and open and closed and those windows that never fucking open and that big bed that holds me naked, that person, who is she? Where is she? Is she in too deep? Does it matter how well you do most of the time if at that very last minute you scream and kick your family out of an almost moving car as they sob? Tell them to watch their hands as the big metal of the door slams and mutes their cries? The answer is no. Seventy-eight dollars and the tank is full, I pull the lever and it just can't take anymore, I'm in too deep now, there's no way out. The answer is no. Damn that shit's expensive, I say to you, and you nod and we laugh, knowing we both don't mind the price to stand here along these sounds and have each other to look at and away from again and again.

SOLVE FOR WAYS TO DISAPPEAR

Alysia Li Ying Sawchyn

A word problem:

Alysia packs two suitcases. She boards a westward-bound plane with an average cruising speed of 570 mph, leaving behind one ex-boyfriend, one cat, and one current boyfriend. If the plane flies continuously for 7.45 hours, and if Alysia stays in the city of her final destination for four months, loses ten pounds, and starts sleeping with another ex, how much closer to happiness will she be than when she first arrived through immigration? Please show your work in the blank space below.

*

In the Low Countries, the clackety-clack of metro trains running through narrow tunnels comes to a violent stop during the wintertime because the sun disappears for days, and so the suicide rate rises and throwing human bodies—sacks of meat and bone—in front of fast-moving trains becomes an accepted method of chosen death.

*

At dinner, the Belgian family I lived with could not recall the name of Picasso's art movement. They tossed words back and forth with rolling r's and nasally vowels, and my slipped-in *Cubisme*, the i sound stretched and long, like I belonged in their capital city, made them look at me with different eyes. Like I'd been hiding a rare gem behind my collarbones.

*

Another type of death is sleeping with men with mouths like heroin. Hands, too. This is to say that they did it, or say they did, or still do, or that being with them feels like nodding out.

*

I said *November, November* and meant it, but then November came and I was not home; the plane ticket I'd had all along was dated December 11th. I was asked in November by the acquaintance who'd agreed to watch my cat until that month, *What should we do with him?* I shrugged across two thousand miles, asked the ex I'd left behind, *What should we do with the stupid cat you bought to prove a point, the cat neither of us wanted but I kept because you couldn't care for it?* He didn't know either. The cat—Achilles, the warrior—has a new home, happier now without either of us.

*

When the current boyfriend I left behind let me go I felt light, weightless.

Rather than floating or drifting, I hurled my body in different directions until something caught or I stuck. Any attachment was better than none, at least for a little while. And then the attachment became a heavy weight, so heavy. Pick a starting point on the Cartesian plane, pick an endpoint straight down, the slope of a line so steep it is undefined; find me at the bottom.

*

My bedroom window overlooked terra-cotta rooftops. The gray sky came down to rub itself across the burnt red and orange tiles. I imagined my no-longer cat running across them like wild smoke. Prescient, Cheshire-like, he grinned, said, *Some go this way, some go that, but I myself prefer the shortcut.*

*

One day, I ran for the train and its doors caught me without slowing. My body slammed between two opposing forces that then opened with a languor that seemed comical in contrast. I remember neither where I was going or why I was rushing, only my bruised shoulders and how the orange plastic seats were so bright they made the city's grime more apparent.

*

I have another boyfriend again. I even have another cat that matches the color of the winter Belgian skies and is as skittish as the sun on those short days. But at night I still dream about the man with a heroin mouth. In my dream we are together, and he is kissing a woman either through or behind a shower curtain. It's a fractal pattern, a splintering crystal. Look through this facet: I am at peace, existing solidly in a space, in my body.

IT'S EXACTLY WHAT YOU THINK

Matthew E. Henry

H e caught the last thirty minutes of the original *Stepford Wives* in a motel two days ago. And while "pod people" is an expression he knows, *The Invasion of the Body Snatchers* holds more historical meanings to his mind, ones that seem suddenly relevant. He's only taken a few steps inside—could turn around and walk out the open diner door—but his legs are car-tired and he hasn't eaten anything of substance for at least four hundred miles. Looking around, he can hear his sister's voice in his head: "This is some WWPS." Weird white people shit. She wouldn't be wrong.

It's not that being watched is unusual. He's a Black man between the ages of eleven and death. The white gaze is as familiar to him as breathing, and reading white eyes is a finely honed survival tactic. His mind is a filing system for the various furtive glances and aggressive stares. He knows the statements swimming through the base of the reptilian brain. Can actually hear what they're thinking, clear as a haunted house's first warning.

"*This* is the doctor?!" is common on first visits to his practice, identifies those who read his qualifications and only glanced at his name without searching for his picture. Obviously, "Is he going to steal something?" is

common in stores. When looking especially present-
able, there's the lilt of a young woman's "Hello," followed
by the forceful "Not on my watch!" from the mother
suddenly grasping her arm, placing a terrified body
between them. There's a subtle shade between "What's
he doing here?" and the unintelligible gasps when
they're surprised at his presence, too close or existing
at all. These are always made more interesting by the
accompanying action. The clutched purse or pearls.
The becoming one with an elevator wall. His favorite
is the sudden remembrance of something important,
somewhere else, requiring a quick exit: a wallet left
in a restaurant, a kettle whistling on the stove, a baby
sinking into the bathtub. Then, of course, there are the
violent gradations of "You don't belong here!" But this
is weird: these eyes aren't hostile, at least not exactly.
More like something out of *The Twilight Zone*, though
he's only seen the reboot by the guy who wrote *Get Out*.

He's always been up for adventure, different ways to
satiate his wanderlust. But when driving cross country,
there's no Black TripAdvisor to help avoid sundown
communities. And he's yet to figure out how to upgrade
his Google Maps to label places that commemorate
lynching trees. So he's learned a few tricks over the
years. He stopped in this town, entered this quaint family
diner, because it seemed safe. A somewhat metropolitan
suburb in a purple state, with more Subaru Outbacks
and Priuses on the road than he ever saw in Seattle. BLM
and #Resist bumper stickers signal from the majority
of the vehicles he passes. Most houses display both a
rainbow-colored "In this house we believe..." and an
oversized "Hate has no home here" sign on their lawn.
It's inviting enough for a twenty-minute pit stop.

By his fourth step toward the counter, every head turns, every set of eyes is tracking him. Every single one. Families, couples, single diners. Everyone. But it's not like those movies where a dark stranger walks into a room, the music screeches to a stop, and the whole place goes dead-cricket silent. Ashlie-RaeAnn Gemington is still crooning her latest hit through hidden speakers, a little too loud for so small a space. The murmur of conversations and laughter have not halted for one moment. The people are still talking to each other, on their phones and, as evidenced by the old, disheveled man in the corner, to themselves. But their eyes are locked on him. Every time he moves, their eyes follow him, but their heads stay at an exact, acute tilt. Each shows too much white around dilated pupils and stunning irises of bright blue and green and amber. They're like those paintings he saw during the sixth-grade field trip to that art museum. The one that got robbed. But his mind drifts to an episode of the show *Supernatural,* until he sees a woman shake salt onto her hash browns, her eyes on his face.

This is not his first time drowning in a sea of whiteness. He smiles back, gives a downward nod to the family at the table he's passing. He gets no response. Or, if the father did nod back, it was minute enough to go unnoticed. But he's no stranger to this brand of polite rudeness. The problem is the silence: he can't hear what their eyes are saying. For the first time in as long as he can remember, he's blocked from their minds. He wonders if it has something to do with their smiles. Each face wears the same expression: a thin, curved line cut in plaster. Or maybe it's alabaster. Whatever that museum's statues were made of. Or that episode of *Doctor Who* with the stone angels playing that fucked-up game of Red Light, Green Light.

But these people aren't getting any closer. Not yet. Just staring with silent eyes and enigmatic smiles. His brother would call it sinister curiosity.

The woman behind the counter is of indeterminate age. Sixteen or twenty-seven or forty-eight: he can't be sure.

As he approaches, her head tilts slightly to the left. Her eyes widen. She leans in toward him. Her face is flawless, but not in a pretty way. She has the same smile as the rest, but it's brighter somehow. More inviting. Like one of the sirens, or...he's beginning to think of a modern example, when he realizes that none of her teeth are showing. He attempts to casually glance behind. None of their teeth are showing. It's table after table of slightly curved, unparted, oddly plump lips. He turns back to the counter and squints, realizing he can't make out the red scribble on her name tag. He simply says hello. She smiles a hint wider. He opens his mouth to order, his finger raising toward the lone, dark blueberry muffin in the display case. Her eyes widen further, showing more white. He thinks she leans in, eyes on his face. He hears... something. Turns. He feels the room has collapsed, everyone millimeters closer, though still talking and laughing. All their eyes still on him. He realizes he's never heard the sound of turning, scraping chairs.

He turns back to the counter, but he's forgotten about the muffin. He sees her mouth is beginning to open, slowly, a growing gleam of white from between too pink lips. His neck begins to tingle. Her eyes... He can almost hear a whisper forming in his mind, but he can't quite make it out. Slowly, carefully, he backs out of the diner, wide eyes and white teeth imperceptibly following him the whole way to the open door.

THE GIRL WITH A PAINTED TONGUE

Tara Isabel Zambrano

The girl in my class paints her tongue with a different color every day. When I see her, she sticks out her tongue—blue, yellow, lavender. It's rude to do that, I say, and she does it again. In class, she sits on the last bench and I can feel her eyes on my back. When I turn around, she's not there. The teacher takes a roll call, and someone says, Yes, when her name is called.

The girl has unusually long legs and arms, her palms are also painted. Smooth, no lifeline, no marks. She carries a mirror with her, uses it to focus light and burn bugs. When she laughs, language falls out on the ground like pebbles shaking with sound.

In my dreams, the girl plucks my eyelashes and makes a string. She inserts the string in my mouth, says she's pulling out my soul because she doesn't have one. I wake up out of breath, my hand over my chest, my heart so loud I get a headache. When I tell my classmates about the dream, they push me and laugh, call me crazy. Watching from a corner, the girl sticks the tip of her tongue out.

When I instruct the girl to stop appearing in my dreams, she claims she has no control, moving the mirror in her hand, flickering light around me, making me dizzy. I cannot stop, she says in her singsong voice. Cannot. Stop.

Go away, I yell. She shakes her head and pushes the mirror in the pocket of her overalls. What do you want? I ask.

I want to play with you, she says. Her tongue is oxblood red like the Indian goddess Kali. She pulls out a doll from her pocket. Blond hair, brown eyes, black wool dress. This doll can talk, she says and hands it to me. Is that so? The doll looks at me, sticks out her tongue. I almost drop it. You can have her, the girl says. No, it's fine, I say, and throw the doll on the floor. The doll gets up and floats in the air, raises her hands. Her palms are painted.

Shit, I scream, and run to my class. The girl and the doll follow me, disappear when I run inside the room. Everyone is looking at me, whispering. The girls who pushed me are giggling. The teacher makes me stand in the corner for being late. She asks me why my palms are painted.

After school, when the bus comes, the girl with the painted tongue is back. She sits behind me, quiet. Then she passes me a bag of tortilla chips, flaming hot, my favorite. I look away as if I don't know her and continue licking my palms to get rid of the color. She whispers in my ear that she's having a party and I should come. I'm the only friend she's got. I think of all the times I've wanted to have friends, when I wanted someone to invite me to their birthday. Tears stream down my face. I turn around and look at her.

Where's your doll?

I threw her away because she bothered you, the girl says. Her eyes soft and wet. We are rounding up a mountain. The bus is close to the edge, almost flying. This isn't the way to my home, but it's beautiful wherever we are going. The valley below is filled with trees with painted leaves, little tongues hanging out. She pulls out the mirror and faces it toward me. I stick my tongue out. In my reflection, she does the same.

LEAVE ME IN THE SUN

Michael B. Tager

For Mandy, who loved the moon

I n Arizona, we decided to leave the I-70 and head south. The roof was down, the sun was high, and I knew I wouldn't get this close to the border for a long time, maybe ever, and for whatever reason, I needed to. Viv didn't care and said so, so long as we stopped off and got something to drink. Not high-alcohol beer—we didn't want to get drunk—but something cool that reminded us we weren't ready to die.

Viv pulled off the first exit we saw and vaguely followed signs that promised civilization. I watched the sky. Vultures circling in the distance, a hawk floating on air currents looking for all the world like a lazy kid on a boogie board drifting in the Atlantic. "Wouldn't it be nice to be a bird?"

"I don't know. What kind of gas mileage do they get?"

"A thousand miles to the gallon," I said without pause.

"Sounds like a good deal," she said. Viv didn't always pay attention. That was okay, I didn't really need her to validate me. Sometimes I just wanted to say words and have them evaporate.

Eventually we came upon a small town—Jackson's Corner—and slowed down. A lot of the houses had white picket fences and satellite dishes. All the cars were better than ours, too. It looked like it was just the one street, but I didn't understand Arizona and I couldn't judge anything without tall buildings. I was too much of the city.

We skidded to a stop outside a little adobe hut-looking store that advertised Budweiser in big red letters. "What does it look like, Teddy?"

I scratched my nose and winced. Was I starting to burn? Viv wore a hat to hide her pale skin. I wished I'd worn a hat. I wondered if beer would make things worse instead of better. It usually did. "It looks delightful."

It was cool inside, and cramped. Beers stacked to the ceiling. Mostly name brands, nothing I would normally drink, but it's good to not be so choosy and snobby sometimes. There were a couple customers, big white men with beer guts and massive biceps. One of them had a little kid following him, freckled and clutching a stuffed bunny. The teller was white, too, and he gave Viv a long look. I could see his brain churning, wondering what a Chinese girl was doing out here. Joke was on him though. Viv was born in Jersey, just like her parents. Her uncle had been a city councilman.

We grabbed a case of Budweiser and a case of Heineken, and a bunch of jerky and some potato chips. I got a couple bottles of water and for some reason we decided that we needed some whiskey. Who we thought was going to drink all of this was beyond me, but we were almost forty and that's reason enough.

While we waited in line, one of the men sidled up to Viv and said hello. He was handsome, with round cheeks and just the right amount of stubble. Viv looked him up and down and grinned. "You just passing through?" he asked.

"That's right."

"You shouldn't. There's a dance out at Mickey's. Got a band and everything. It'll be a hoot." He licked his lips and leaned in a little, testing the waters. When Viv took a step back, he took a step back, too. That's always nice to see.

"I like dances and I like hoots," Viv said. "But we have someplace to be."

The man glanced at me and nodded, tipping his trucker hat. It said Dallas on it. Not very exciting, but it reminded me of my own needs so I glanced around and lo and behold, right by the door was a bunch of hats. Hot damn. I walked on over while Viv and the man flirted their asses off. If this was ten, fifteen years ago, Viv probably could have been convinced. She'd been that sort. She was from Jersey.

I came back to the line just as the teller was ringing everything up. The handsome man was nowhere to be seen. "Where did your friend go?" I asked Viv. I tossed the hat on the counter. It was camo and had a deer on it. I didn't like hunting but any port in a storm. "And this."

Viv shrugged and handed the cashier her credit card. "Pack of cigarettes too."

"What kind?" His voice was raspy and soft. Like a supervillain.

"It really doesn't matter." She turned to me. "He had to go. He gave me his number. That was cute."

The teller threw a pack of Camels and matches into the bag with the jerky and the chips and we were off. I put the hat on and admired myself in the mirror. I cracked open one of the Buds and took a sip, grimaced, and took a gulp. "You going to call him?"

"Hell no," she said as she turned the car on. "His name is Gerald. I can't sleep with a Gerald."

I thought it was a pretty fair point. "He seemed nice."

"He was nice. It's not his fault that's his name, but here we are. And there he is, named Gerald. Light me one of those cigarettes, would you?"

I said sure and hid from the wind as she accelerated. The matches kept on going out and I cursed, but eventually I got one going for her, and then another for me. It tasted disgusting, but I kept smoking and I kept on drinking the Budweiser until we got back to the highway. When it was gone, I cracked open another. It felt right in the sun.

Eventually night came and the moon rose like a big white space rock. It was enormous, hanging so low its belly seemed to drag on the mountains in the distance. I was on my eighth beer. Viv was on her third. I didn't feel drunk but I probably was, even though I'd also gone through three bottles of water. God, I had to pee, but neither of us felt like stopping. Especially with the moon looking like that. I pointed at her and said to Viv, "You ever think about the moon?"

Viv took a drag and exhaled into the night. The smoke looked like a plum, then like a dragon, then like smoke again. Viv's chest was flushed from the drinking. She just had on a tank top. I had a white T. And my hat, of course. Can't forget my hat. I wished I'd worn a tank top.

"I wish I'd worn a tank top," I said.

"Don't you have one in your bag? Go get it."

"I look terrible in tank tops," I said.

"Who do you have to impress out here?" She laughed and asked for another beer.

"Her," I said, pointing at the moon. "I feel like it's a trap and she'll judge me if I wear something unflattering."

Viv chewed her lip and took her eyes off the road long enough to drink it all in. I could see the moon in her right iris; I couldn't see her left but I suspected the moon was there, too. Viv seemed to change then, like her soul started to escape through her nostrils, like the heavy magnetic tension that was our destination started to evaporate. At the end of this drive was Pittsburgh and her new job, and then Baltimore and my spouse and my kids. She didn't really want the job. I wanted my family, but I didn't want them right now, and I didn't want them all the time.

Finally, Viv snorted and said, "Sweetie, you're a weird one. You know that, right?"

I did know that, so I held up my beer and we cheersed and I kept on watching the moon until I fell asleep and when I woke, Viv was on the side of the road peeing in the starlight and I said, "That sounds like a really, really good idea," so I joined her and we just pissed into the desert like some old-timey folks. It felt nice.

"Your turn to drive."

"I'm a little drunk."

"It's a straight line. Just don't swerve."

I adjusted my seat, and I turned on the radio but there was nothing on. I told Viv to put on some music so she pulled up some kind of techno on her phone—that's what I get for not being specific—but I felt pretty good from napping, so I lit a cigarette as I got back on the road and accelerated. I ate some jerky. I'd be a vegetarian again when I got home.

Viv was soon snoring. I felt refreshed as hell. Hadn't felt this good in a long time, really. Must be the beer, or the nicotine, or the jerky, or maybe it was just being outside with a friend and free of everything, even for a short time. It was snowing in Baltimore. I couldn't believe it. Right now I was cold, because we were in the desert and night sand retains no heat or memory, but I remembered the sweat, and my burned skin certainly remembered the sun. Sometimes I wish I could just be left at the beach to melt. When things are left out in the sun, they return to their essence. They rot or they are eaten, they are melted or they are turned to vapor.

"What do you think it would be like?" I asked my sleeping friend. "For the sun to bleach our bones and tan our skin? Do you think it would hurt? I think it would be like coming home again. I think it would be like being born."

Viv said nothing. She snored a little louder and shivered in her sleep. I put the roof up and grabbed her phone to turn the music down. No more thumpa-thumpa-thumpa. Tomorrow would be another day. I ate more jerky and drank more water and just drove. I'd make good vapor. I was sure of it.

"Where are we?" Viv eventually asked. The sun was back out and the roof was back down. The back floor was littered with jerky wrappers and an empty bag of salt 'n' vinegar chips. The family-size bag. I don't mess around with chips.

"Texas. It's a big-ass sky out here." I indicated the world. There was scrubland for days and mountains in the distance. Or maybe they were big hills. It's splitting hairs but mountains are mountains and hills are hills. Language is imprecise and life is unpredictable so it's best to get things right whenever you can. You don't call the moon anything but her name. She'd take offense.

"Real big." She stretched and grinned at the enormous blue above her. It wasn't yet hot. "What time is it?"

I shrugged and avoided looking at the clock on the dash. Time was not what I wanted to think about. "Your phone has been buzzing a lot," I said by way of misdirection. I was a magician. Ta da.

She yawned and readjusted her hat and checked her phone. She grunted and I could see her thin fingers touching and scrolling and expanding and shrinking. What was she doing? Was she checking all of the social media? Posting all of the things? Texting with the world?

I hadn't checked my phone in two days. I was positive my spouse had called and sure my friends had sent me GIFs of cats and memes and news of the world. I wasn't interested. I didn't want it. I just wanted this to never end. I wanted to be young again, not in body exactly, but in my brain and soul. I wanted to imagine what my life was going to be like, not wonder if something was missing or if this was all there was.

I asked her what all the commotion was. She grunted and tossed it into the backseat where it clattered against all of the cans just loitering like slackers. Like dead soldiers. She said, "Gerald sent me a bunch of texts."

"Did he really? What did he want? Did he want you to go to the hoot?"

She laughed. "He just asked me about my day and sent pictures of his dogs. A lot of them."

"How many dogs does he have? How many dogs is a lot?" I wondered if it meant anything, someone having a lot of dogs. Maybe people have more dogs in Arizona 'cause of all the room to wander. But weren't there coyotes and weren't they a problem when it came to pets? I know a lot of outside cats were killed by coyotes.

Probably not a bad thing, considering how bad cats were. In Australia, they're killing all of the native fauna. Cats are dicks. I had three and I loved them, but I was under no illusions about their sweetness.

"A lot of pictures, not a lot of dogs. I think he has two." She stretched and asked to pull over soon to find some place to wash up. We were going to drive mostly straight on through, but we still needed to be humans. California to Pittsburgh is too long to not brush your teeth.

Not long after, she pointed at a sign that advertised Big Bend National Park. "Rio Grande is there," she said. "Let's stretch our legs."

In the parking lot, we dumped all of the beer cans in the trash. A family of four with Utah license plates watched us. The man had this pinched expression like he hadn't taken a dump in six years. His wife had dark moles. Their kids were cute and one of them waved at me. Maybe they were Mormons.

There was a visitor center where we changed our undies and brushed our teeth in the bathroom. Then we found a path and walked south. I had a couple beers in a plastic bag and Viv had the jerky and the cigarettes and a big bottle of water. We passed the supplies back and forth and ignored all the looks we got from the families and the old people and even the ranger. We were on vacation. We were recapturing our youth and pretending that the future wasn't encroaching upon us. Give us a break.

Eventually we came to the river and walked on the shore. I waded in up to my knees and felt an inexorable pull east. The water was cool and for a moment I felt peaceful, but I knew it was just the calming effects of nature. It wouldn't last.

We sat on the bank. A few other tourists walked past us, over us, through us, around us, but we didn't acknowledge any of them. I put my arm around her and she leaned into me.

When the sun was directly overhead, threatening, I said, "Maybe we should go."

Viv said, "I wish we could just stay in this moment forever. Like, I'm leaving here for *Pittsburgh?*"

"I hear they have good pierogis?"

"What does that have to do with anything? Who cares about pierogis?"

I shrugged. "I don't know. An ex told me about a pierogi pizza they had in Pittsburgh. Said it was the best thing they'd ever eaten. I've always wanted to try it out."

She scratched her nose and hmphed and then helped me to my feet. We walked back to the visitor center and went to the bathroom and got back into the car. We drove for another day and night, and then we left Texas. We ate at roadside taco stands and greasy diners and any place that wasn't a chain and didn't look likely to judge us for being by ourselves and not being bathed. For wearing novelty trucker hats proclaiming "I drink because of you." For being lost adults. For having souls and bodies and half-empty gas tanks.

We left Texas and drove through Louisiana. Viv wanted to turn north and get back on route, back to I-70, back to the vein masquerading as a road, because the path was faster and easier that way, but I said, "No, let's stick with the sun. Let's go to Florida." I didn't want to explain why I needed this, didn't want to acknowledge that adding days of travel was the point, didn't want Viv or anyone to know that delaying the return to reality wasn't a strategy to achieve a goal, it was the goal itself, it was the destination, it was what's worth seeking.

I appreciated that, with Viv, I didn't need to make my case. If she needed more info, she'd ask, and then she would either agree or she wouldn't, and that would be the end of it. I didn't need to plead my case, and thank God for that, because the last thing I wanted was more decisive moments. I wanted to decide nothing. I wanted to be aggressively apathetic. I wanted Viv to drive, and I wanted the sun to make my decision and for the moon to use me as canvas.

Viv checked the schedule and said, "Well fine," and we kept on going.

As we got closer, I got quieter. I didn't want to leave the sun or where I could drive under the moon with the top down and feel her kissing my hair, and I didn't want to drive past Baltimore on the way. Viv was going to be the vice president of a bank. She was going to move into a condo on the tenth floor and she was going to go to bed at night after looking out her window at the sleeping valley beneath her. She was going to be good at her job. They'd asked her to come, she hadn't applied. It was an honor. She wanted to retire with this job. She'd told me that when she'd asked me to come to help her pack and move everything she owned across the country. It's the kind of thing you can ask the friend you met at a swim meet in the third grade. It's the kind of thing you say yes to.

I think my family understood when I told them I was leaving. The kids definitely did. They could never sit still and they knew I was like them, even as I was forced by them to always remain frozen. They loved tag, they loved to yell "Freeze." They knew I chafed, but I did it because I love them, and they always let me go as soon as they could. Kids get it. They knew I'd be back.

We stopped at the Everglades and wandered around the park, looking at the crocodiles ("They're alligators," Viv kept reminding me) and marveling at how very swampy it was. We stopped in Savannah and put on our light jackets from the trunk and had BBQ on the river. We stopped in Asheville and listened to aged hippies play the music of their youth. We put on gloves and put the top up in Virginia. Near Baltimore, Viv said she'd drop me off.

"No," I said. "I want to be there when you see your new place. I want to help you unload all your possessions from the pod. I want to look at the moon from your condo and I want to see the sun come up. Don't you understand?"

She looked at me with a crinkle in her forehead. She had more lines than the last time I saw her, which is to say three years ago, or was it five? I had more, too. I was going to be fine once I got home. But right now, right in this moment, I was far from okay. I was letting the weakness in because sometimes I needed space to be weak. I'm asked to be strong all day long in real life and that just makes you brittle.

Right now, in this moment, I took her right hand off the wheel and held it. She smiled and squeezed. On some level, she got it. I was glad I didn't have to say it out loud. It would lose its power if I put it into words.

We passed Baltimore. It was blanketed in snow still and I wondered how everyone was doing. I hadn't looked at my phone in days. I didn't feel bad about it. Viv was posting pictures and all from the road. My spouse followed her and I'm sure saw everything and knew I was okay.

We left Maryland and the sun set. The moon was smaller here, the stars hidden. It was still beautiful. It still called my name and threatened a good time. I offered to drive and Viv said no, that she was fine. She lit two cigarettes and handed one to me. We put the windows down and blew the smoke out and I said, here you go God, here you go Moon, take my soul.

Pennsylvania stretched long and we drove through the night, until we pulled up to a tall building where she would live. It was the wee hours and the night watchman gave us a long look when we strolled in. I knew what he saw. I knew how greasy my gray hair was, how much the sweat on me had dried and what days of poor ventilation did. So did Viv. But she was always so good at not caring. I'd learned from her.

"I live here," she said. "Tenth floor. Chen." The night man nodded and wrote her name on a form and explained that they'd been expecting her two days earlier, that her pod was in the parking garage. She said, "We lost track of time." He said he understood. I wondered if he did. He was older than us.

We were quiet on the elevator. Her phone buzzed and she chuckled when she looked at it. "Gerald again," she said, showing me a picture of him holding his dog in his arms, the sky and the sun behind him. His face was in shadow.

"You going to invite him to visit?" I asked.

"God no," she said. "He's just a nice man who likes to text." Which was true, I supposed.

Viv's condo was quiet and cold and mostly empty. But there was a couch and an easy chair and in the spare room there was a bed. Condos all came with a little bit of furniture. That was nice of them.

We sat and I instantly felt how bone-crushingly tired I was. "I'm going to miss you," I said. "This has been…"

"Yeah," she said, "it's been."

"I'm glad you've moved nearby. I've really missed you." She put her strong arms around me and crushed my shoulder blades as she squeezed. I felt them turn into dust and my organs burst and a few tears slid out, but I hid those. I wanted her to be happy.

"How long has it been since we've been friends?" she asked. When I told her, she said, "It doesn't feel like it's been that long. It really doesn't."

"Why?"

"Because we have so much left to say to each other. We never run out."

I told her it was true and we hugged again and then she got up to get some stuff from her car. At the door she turned and told me that she loved me. "I love you too, man," I said.

"More than the moon?"

"Fuck no," I said. "But more than anyone else."

Alone in the condo, I opened cupboards and cabinets. They were empty, as expected, so I walked over to the big windows facing east and I opened the blinds, hoping to catch the sunrise. "Well, aren't I lucky?" I said, because there was the just the hint of sun coming up, a burnt orange peeking out over the horizon, like a kid playing hide and seek. And still high in the sky, ruling it like a queen, there was the moon.

I sighed and leaned my head against the glass and wondered what it would be like to be a bird, high up in the sky, on a first-name basis with the sun and moon and everything in between. Would it be like I thought it was? It couldn't be. But maybe.

A few moments went by before I shook my head. I looked at the moon and burgeoning sun. I rested my head against the glass. I let my life come back to me.

LINES OF COMMUNICATION

Miriam Gershow

The marital therapist said they need to establish new lines of communication, so Carla started making Edgar rebus puzzles. The first one was easy:

"I see you?" Edgar said at the breakfast table before he left for campus. She'd made him oats, steel cut. He said his answer after having studied the rebus for a very long time.

"Yes!" she said. "I see you, Edgar."

"Thank you," Edgar said.

I see you was incorrect, but Carla didn't have the heart. The answer was "I am inside of you" or "I am a part of you." She would have accepted either.

She'd planned to follow it with the inverse—

—which now she'd have to forgo. It was okay to forgo, she told herself. Marriage was an improvisation; it was making and remaking.

The next one, a sentence:

🐑 👨‍🦰–s m+ 👁 ♥,

🕯 🐑+r 🌿 n+ ◻

Edgar studied the rebus over dinner. Carla had made chicken tika masala, her go-to from their trip to southern India years earlier. This replaced her gazpacho, her previous go-to from their trip to Portugal years even earlier.

"Canned tomatoes?" Edgar said, pressing the back of his fork into the chicken.

She had wanted to tell him "Ewe r knot careful" but she couldn't come up with a rebus for careful. *Nice* was close enough, and also true.

"We shave the sheep with a seeing heart butt?" he said after a long time. He was joking, and at his own expense, which was unusual for Edgar. His joking was usually about everyone else.

Edgar wasn't good at the rebus puzzles. Carla liked this about Edgar. Edgar was a professor of history. He was the leading scholar of pre-industrial Hungary in the world. Edgar knew more about pre-industrial Hungary than all the people of Hungary.

When the marital therapist checked in about the new lines of communication, Carla said, "Great!" She loved coming up with the rebuses. They made her brave. She wished the marital therapist had suggested this years earlier, though they hadn't had a marital therapist years earlier, the marital therapist only coming into play when the PhD student in pre-industrial Hungary (They existed? They existed!) sent the text in the middle of the night, Edgar deaf to it from behind his CPAP machine, Carla the one to see the three words.

"Edgar?" the marital therapist said now. The marital therapist often had to say Edgar's name for Edgar to speak.

"I don't—" Edgar said. Edgar looked out the window. Carla turned to look. It was only a tree.

On their trip to Portugal years earlier, the boys had been so little, and Carla hadn't spoken Portuguese (still didn't). So much of the vacation had been wrangling and herding and comforting and coaxing while only having a half sense of what was happening around her, a half sense of the beautiful churches she was supposed to be admiring, a half sense of the cobblestones that Edgar kept remarking upon, and not because the boys kept tripping and scraping their knees and the pads of their palms, but because the history of cobblestone in southern Europe, Edgar wanted them to know, was really a very interesting story.

One morning over scrambled egg whites (had to watch Edgar's high cholesterol), she handed him:

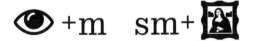

and he knit his brow and shrugged and it occurred to her maybe he wasn't bad at rebuses. Maybe he wasn't trying. That night on his pillow she wrote him:

+r a +e

He looked before giving a *ffh* and moving it off the pillow like one might an interloping katydid or a hotel dinner mint, not roughly, but clearing the way for the business of a pillow. He was not trying. It had been a test, the easiest rebus yet. Edgar was many things, but not a bully. Had he given it more than half a glance, he would have protested, Edgar exquisitely attuned to injustice toward himself. Instead, he kissed Carla on the corner of her lip and strapped himself into his CPAP.

At the restaurant in Portugal—she remembered it exactly, tiny, dark walls, sconces, a handsome waiter with dark skin and dark hair—it was the second to last night, the boys exactly the right amount of tired and at the same time, sedate in their chairs, an event as rare and notable as an eclipse, the end of the trip near enough for Carla to be buoyed from her exhaustion and disappointment and unshakable sense that everything was impossible and she was getting it all wrong. When the handsome waiter set down the soup, and she tasted her first taste, the gazpacho moved her in ways she didn't know she could be moved by soup. She'd never had anything like it: cold, sharp, dense, spicy, smooth. It had filled her.

Carla stopped saying anything except for rebuses to see if Edgar noticed. At breakfast:

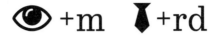 +m +rd

Two days later, before bed:

 f+ –d

The marital therapist checked in. Carla let Edgar go first. Edgar shrugged. "I don't—"
"You don't what?" the marital therapist asked.
Edgar shrugged.
"I said lettuce fuck and he ignored me," Carla said.
"What?" Edgar said. "What are you—?"
"What disinterests you about making love to Carla?" the marital therapist asked Edgar.
"She never said!" Edgar said, exquisitely attuned. "She never!"

There'd been a crystalline moment in Portugal, Carla nearly finished with the gazpacho but not quite, she slowing to savor the last of it, even then knowing to slow down for the good things when they came, and she took in her husband and her boys in the half-lit tableau of the restaurant, half a world away from home and thought: All this for a guileless gal from Sioux Falls, who'd gone bananas for her Intro to World History TA, he so handsome and sophisticated, she so fat with his first baby before she could see the other side of sophomore year. What she felt was lucky and grateful and full.

She made him his goulash for dinner, his favorite. Edgar pronounced it gulyás, always, so many gulyáses over so many years. "Good," he proclaimed (gulyás, if it hit Edgar at the right moment, made him expansive), "girl."

Tonight she had a single question.

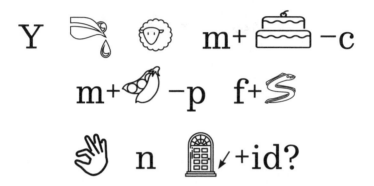

"The sheep," Edgar said. "Always with the sheep. Good to see we're letting it eat cake now. And peas. And allowing it an eel."

She'd tried with gazpacho over a number of years, well past when she understood gazpacho to be exotic or even particularly novel. For years, the issue was too much garlic and then not enough garlic, followed by a period of "vinegar" and "more vinegar" until finally, one night Edgar said "Uch," at a first, vinegary spoonful. The boys had found that funny, the noise and their father's screwed-up face. They weren't so young by then, old enough to know better, but excited utterances were not like their father, displays of emotion either. Carla watched Edgar, seeing his dawning surprise. He hadn't meant to clown, but his face bloomed at the boys' reaction, tickled and pleased with himself, as if realizing for the first time these were not shrunken men at the table, but children, and his. He screwed his face even screwier. "Uch!" he said loudly. "This is terrible soup!" and the three of them laughed.

Carla had a rebus in her head for a long time. First it was:

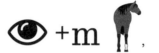

which she knew was too obscure for Edgar—or anyone. It didn't matter. It was a secret to herself. Eventually, it turned into

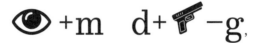

which Edgar could understand, were he willing. She pictured Edgar finding the rebus on the table and waiting for his breakfast and wondering what was taking so long, getting up from the table and backtracking to the bedroom to be sure she wasn't still there, hidden beneath the blankets, Edgar calling her name, peeking in half-open bathroom doors. "Carla!" he would call, a scratch to his voice, his throat always dried out in the morning from the CPAP. She pictured Edgar returning to the table, flummoxed, picking up the paper for the first time, really studying it.

She pictured and pictured this for so long, she thought she would keep picturing it after. She thought it would become the crystalline moment of her next era, since she had no way of knowing the next era would be taken up by entirely new things—a zing of chili in her dark chocolate, a Pomeranian with an incontinence problem but such a sweet face, a dwarf bonsai she knew to keep humid from the very detailed instructions, so she spritzed and spritzed it dutifully and happily, several times a day.

BEFORE THE BIG BANG

Kelsey Francis

I am not supposed to leave the bed. A nurse tells me that if I need to use the bathroom, I should press the little red button on the palm-sized wand.

"It'll buzz me, hon," she says and pats my hand where an IV is taped. A slow drip of Pitocin is working its way through my veins, silently communicating to my uterus in an ancient language translated by a pharmaceutical company. But my uterus isn't listening.

A long, three-inch-wide band of elastic is stretched around the middle of my belly, swollen to its maximum nine-month size. The elastic is an equatorial line, holding a fetal monitor transducer tightly in place. Cords and tubing and electrodes tether me to the bed, inside this room, in this corner of a hospital, in this neck of the woods, in this region of the state, in this part of the country, on this edge of the world.

My husband is downstairs in the parking garage. His pants' pockets are full of loose quarters. I had teased him the night before: "You aren't fifteen and going to the boardwalk with a video arcade. It's a maternity ward. We're having a baby."

But he brought the quarters anyway.

"Maybe there will be a jukebox. You never know— you might want to dance," he had said. He took my hand

and spun me around the kitchen floor, a pregnant lady in orbit, and we laughed.

But that was before today. When we could make stupid jokes about pockets full of loose quarters and maternity wards with video arcades and jukeboxes. When we spoke with certainty about the future.

I can picture my husband, his pockets full of silver, wandering deeper and deeper into a dark concrete abyss. He is lost and can't remember on what level our car is parked, where the forgotten phone charger sits coiled inside a cup holder. There are now so many phone calls to make. So many people to tell.

Before my husband left for the parking garage, a doctor told us that sometimes this *just happens* and we may never learn why. Words left his mouth, but only a splinter-sized piece of me was listening. I was staring at the black and gray monitor screen. There was no woosh-woosh sound while the machine slowly unfurled a long strip of paper with nothing but a straight line. No bumps or wrinkles. No hiccups or dips. No burps or breaks. No peaks or valleys. The line was perfectly smooth, still. Like water. Like glass. Like space.

The doctor then said something about letting the Pitocin do its job and a socialworkeranddoyouwanto talktoaministerandyouwonthavetopayforparkingandIll bebacktocheckonyouinalittlewhile and don't forget to push the little red button if you need to pee.

I don't know why I'm still hooked up to the fetal monitor, so after the doctor leaves the room, and after my husband voyages to the parking garage, I loosen the Velcro of the elastic equator around my belly and watch as it drops to the floor. I rip off the surgical tape holding the IV on my right hand and yank the tube out.

I do not push the little red button.

The tubes, wires, cords, bands, and straps now lie in a tangled mess on the floor. A ball of chaos. They are a useless and lifeless mass without me attached to them. I kick the ball with my bare foot and it disappears underneath a white sheet hanging off the edge of the bed.

I slip off my maternity-size hospital gown and put on my street clothes. I know what the doctors and nurses and my husband don't know. You see, I know they're wrong. Nothing has *happened*. Everything is *fine*. Their monitors and wires and transducers and Pitocin have no idea what is going on inside my body. They don't know about the silent stretching and expanding that happens just before a universe is born.

It's easy for me to walk out of my hospital room and down the hall in sweatpants, sneakers, and an oversized T-shirt. They don't really want me on this floor anyway; I overheard two nurses talking just outside my room about moving me to the cardiac unit, far away from other laboring mothers. *That's right, put me with the broken hearts* I said to myself. I think they were afraid of my screams. But I haven't screamed at all. I've been perfectly calm and silent.

I ride the elevator down four floors and exit into a bright glass atrium four stories tall. It's lunchtime and people dressed in blue or green scrubs are walking quickly across squeaky waxed floors carrying foil-wrapped sandwiches and cardboard cups of soup. There is only so much time to eat before the next emergency.

The invisible electric eye of the sliding doors sees my stomach before my feet have even reached the threshold. The doors open for me and a gust of cool air blows a cloud of fine dust particles into my eyes, lifts up the front of my T-shirt just a bit, exposing a glowing crescent smile of skin to the bright and blinding noonday sun.

BLUEPRINT FOR AN ELOPEMENT

Megha Nayar

N ow that you have decided to spend the rest of your life with this man, you should begin planning your grand escape. Let's be prudent—no matter how desperately you hope for a miracle, the only way you two can be united in matrimony is by forfeiting your families. Given that the estrangement is inevitable, you ought to begin preparing for your departure right away.

But before you proceed to design your elopement plan, you must sit down and establish some ground rules for both of you.

For instance, no visible accoutrements on the body. He is one of the "others"—they who must never be spoken to, let alone befriended—and his otherness is conspicuous. In order to keep your duo from being disbanded, in order to keep the disparity of faith hidden from the gatekeepers of honor, you must always strip yourself of all paraphernalia when reuniting in public. Bodily anonymity is a critical component of interreligious affairs. No bindi on your forehead, no cross around his neck. Your language must be strictly neutral too—no utterances invoking gods, neither his nor yours. This disguise will feel unnatural at first, upsetting even, but you must keep calm and carry on. The rewards will far outweigh the discomfort.

That brings us to the second point—no public displays of affection.

It is well understood that romantic love entails an acute longing for bodily congress. But imperiled lovers such as yourselves must walk the tightrope of restraint with unfailing precision. You must resist the urge to entwine your fingers with his, he must withstand the lure of your lips. Ever heard of this thing called six degrees of separation? There could not possibly be more than three degrees in your little town. If caught canoodling in public by someone you know (or someone who knows you), you will promptly be marched off to hell, never to catch sight of each other again. So, keep the lust-o-meter firmly in check.

What about mobile communication? Surely, you use cell phones to ease your longing—with texts and emojis and audio notes, maybe even risqué images. Whatever you do, never share your passcode with anyone, nor ever leave your phone unattended. The safest option would be to delete each one of your interactions afterwards. But if you're the sentimental type who likes to preserve courtship-era pinings for posterity, remember not to back your photos and videos up on your laptop. And if you do, never lend it to anyone—not friends, and definitely not siblings. Keep a handful of excuses handy for when anybody asks to borrow your laptop. Say that the A and T buttons on the keyboard are malfunctioning, for example, or that a long-pending OS update is under way. Keep a perfectly straight face through it all.

Now, on to the workplace. Since your love story was born in a newspaper office, it will be especially difficult to keep it under wraps. Journalists have the uncanny ability to sniff out even the most meticulously guarded secrets. It is one thing to have bankers or school teachers for co-workers; those are usually too bogged down by the vagaries of their own lives to care for the goings-on in others'. But not so *your* colleagues, many of whom are acclaimed for their investigative journalism. You know all too well that when not trailing government scandals, they're busy seeking headlines in the canteen or parking lot. Be extremely careful not to let slip any signs of your romantic affiliation in their presence. Do not linger around each other, but do not act weirdly aloof either. Play it casual. Talk when you have to, the way you would with anyone else, making no more (or less) eye contact than needed. Refrain from ogling one another on Traditional Day in office, when he turns up in a body-hugging kurta churidar and you in your best sari. Peel your eyes away, don't let slip your fantasies. If you sense heat coloring your cheeks, hide behind one of those A3-sized print dummies until the stirrings in your heart subside.

When you've finally reached the stage where you have enough money in the bank to afford being disowned and enough courage in your bones to start life anew, it is time to put the exit protocol in motion. Follow all the steps given below. Do not skip or dilute any step. Keep your face masks on, always. Remind yourself at all times that overconfidence will derail your love train forever.

Six weeks before D-Day, pay a discreet visit to the family court together. File a notice of intended marriage with the registrar. He will ask you to come back after thirty days—the stipulated period during which objections to the union may be entertained. The mention of objections will send shivers racing up your spines, but hold your wits together and wait. Pray, if that helps.

Four weeks before D-Day, join him in visiting his uncle's decrepit warehouse on the outskirts of town. After a fire killed two workers in the basement, the place has been abandoned for fear of hauntings. Nobody ventures there, not even crows. Clean the place up. Stock its rusted lockers with enough provisions—water, packed food, napkins, medicines—to last a week at least.

Now, begin smuggling your essential belongings out of your homes and into the warehouse. Be subtle, both of you. No more than a couple of shirts a day, or a few pairs of socks. Mothers are hawks; if they notice anything amiss, you will be interrogated. So, take only the bare basics. Pick the functional over the ornate. Forget your books, they are too heavy to be lugged around. If forgiven, you will be able to come back for them some day.

Three weeks prior, apply for a fortnight of leave from work (starting on D-Day). Tell your editor you're traveling to your native village for your cousin's wedding. She will believe you, because you have been talking about this fictitious wedding for a while. On his part, your man must also submit a leave application, citing an ardent desire to accompany his parents on a pilgrimage.

Two weeks before D-Day, buy yourselves two spare phones (not smartphones) and two new SIM cards. Memorize these numbers but share them with no one. Keep all of it safely hidden.

A week before D-Day, tell your mother you're feeling nostalgic. Ask her where the old photo albums are kept. While browsing through the Kashmir album, pull out that photo of the four of you boating on the Dal Lake and slip it into your handbag. In case, God forbid, your parents and sibling decide to cut you off, your favorite memory from your favorite holiday is all that will remain of them with you.

Three days before D-Day, sneak into your father's room while he is in the shower. Open his cabinet and extract the brown folder containing all your documents. There are college marksheets in there, and your art certificates, and advanced diplomas of classical dance. Not to forget a laminated A4-sized laurel testifying that you were the best student of journalism at the country's best media school not too long ago. Even if you're condemned to be remembered as a failed daughter, this folder is evidence that there are plenty of other things you've succeeded in at life. Hide it in your cupboard, carefully.

Two days before D-Day, while the family is busy, embark on an olfactory tour of the house. Sniff at everything, absorb every scent—your father's tube of Vicks VapoRub, your mother's hair comb smudged with bhringraj oil, your sibling's T-shirt that reeks of stale sweat. Hug the curtains in the puja room that smells permanently of incense. Tear a page out of the notebook in which your late grandmother used to write her favorite god's name one hundred and eight times every day. Fold the page and save it in your wallet for a keepsake.

Twenty-four hours before D-Day, unlock your mother's almirah with a duplicate key. Open the iron safe where she keeps her jewelry—the code is 9999—and retrieve the leaf-shaped gold pendant and earrings kept in the green velvet case. Your grandmother had left these in your name, to be gifted at your wedding. This is the only part of your rightful inheritance that you will take with you tomorrow. You will be gone before your mother discovers them missing.

Twelve hours before D-Day, pen your farewell letter. Explain that the man you love is the best man you could ever have loved, and that incongruence of faith is not a good enough reason to forsake him. Don't mention his name, of course, but elaborate freely on his virtues. Inform your family that abscondence is not how you would have wanted to step into marital life, but given the animosity between the communities, this is the only way you will get to walk into the future with him. Apologize—not because you have to, but because it will help blunt the impact of your departure, perhaps even assuage some of their fury. Tell them that you hope to come back eventually to touch their feet, because all love, even the forbidden kind, needs the blessings of elders to endure.

On the morning of D-Day, wear your plainest clothes, have your final breakfast with eyes lowered, and leave at the usual hour. Before leaving, slip the farewell letter under your pillow. Switch off your smartphone. Remember to take the other phone, the new SIM, your brown folder, and the gold. Don't say any goodbyes, nor turn around for one last look at the house, or you won't make it. Drag your trembling legs in the direction of the family court, where he will be waiting for you, his heart throbbing in his ears too. Follow him into the magistrate's cabin. Three friends will be present as witnesses—all his, because none of yours would survive the intensity of police interrogation that will invariably follow this elopement. Nod at the three of them politely. When your names are called out, do as directed. Read the papers. Take the oath. Sign your name—there, there, and there. Voilà, the deed is done. You are now man and wife. You may not kiss each other yet—in fact, you may not even hold hands just yet. Wait till the clerk is finished, the friends are thanked, and the mandatory photograph is clicked.

When all the formalities are accomplished, walk up to the main road and summon an auto rickshaw. Get off a kilometer before your final destination. Here begins the walk to his uncle's abandoned warehouse, where you will hide in peace until the people you both love the most finally put their weapons away.

TYPICAL CALLS OF THE RED-TAILED HAWK
Kate Gehan

Windows down, Ellie drove fast and cranked the radio, then drove faster even fastest but it didn't matter—the baby kept screaming in the backseat. Before swooping out of the house she tossed juice, crackers, and coloring books at the older mouselings on her mother-in-law's kitchen floor. *Where are you going, Mama?* they demanded and she had shrieked, *Out to get him quiet!* while her father-in-law offered only a pinched face, disapproving of eight a.m. drama. He hated her, loved only Tyler, who was at some early college class, more likely hooking up/holding down someone new despite promising the last girl was truly the goddamn last. Obviously, they both liked sex—that's how this all started—but Ellie was twenty-three and holy hell this was now years of living with the McPhersons and when she and Tyler had announced the third pregnancy, she begged telepathically to get kicked out because all five of them in one bedroom was insane, but alas. She and Tyler did it in the shower or the car after the kids were asleep and they went out for dates to Dairy Queen for chocolate-dipped cones like they were fourteen—but now she was always breastfeeding and needed the calcium—and Tyler licked her ear and told her they needed to stay put while his parents paid for his school. Her little teething mouse babe wailed louder still, and Ellie's hair flew around so she couldn't see shit, and she was dizzy from sipping vodka at four a.m. to try to get herself back to sleep after hours of comforting another baby and she was mostly certain the distant siren was in the song on the radio. As soon as she could get to the elementary school, her brother would pour coffee for her in his Number One Teacher mug and help for ten minutes, thirty tops, and she could walk alone in the outdoor classroom, pretend to be a kid, sit on the pond dock to examine fish and insects, make careful notes in a sketchbook. In lieu of actual advice, Ellie's brother always said *be your true self* when she called crying about Tyler. If she got to the pond in the woods behind the school, where the water reflects predators in the sky sweeping hypnotic circles, she would name her true self. Instead of leading a high-speed car chase through the center of town—instead of hitting the curb and slamming into the Letters to Santa mailbox—Ellie would handle the wheel with race car driver precision and slice through Main Street with a demon whisper and get to the woods. She would not emerge from the wreckage clutching her child, surrounded by hostile, unhelpful men. Instead of winding up on the town police social media feed red-eyed with crazy hair to become the hot topic of moms' group conversations for endless months, Ellie would rise like a hawk from the field, talons locked securely around what came from her, belonged to her, would always be hers.

TAMMY'S TAMAGOTCHI

Davon Loeb

The girl's Tamagotchi was still alive even though she wasn't. It was evidence, the kids claimed, and is why they never told any adults about it. Tammy's Tamagotchi, they called it, though, they didn't even remember if her name was Tammy, but the alliteration caught on, the way a rumor does—the way this story did. Tammy's Tamagotchi was nailed to an old pine tree in the middle of nowhere—but nowhere was somewhere in the New Jersey Pine Barrens. The loop of her keychain held it there, and sometimes, the kids, when they rode their bikes on backwoods trails into the swelling darkness of some Friday night, between one world and another, the day into the dusk, they said they could hear the Tamagotchi swinging in some gusty wind, the sound of its plastic body scraping against the bark of that old tree, like a body that was just hanging there, in a shadow of itself. And even the cadence of the Tamagotchi's chirp rang in their imaginations, calling out for Tammy still like how Tammy called for someone's help, sometime after she lost her way, when she supposedly ran away, when the New Jersey Pine Barrens found her. The kids shuddered at the thought, the image, the sound, the idea of any kid's death—how it would all grow in their minds, nestle there, and follow them

home—follow them, like how a shadow does—follow
them out of the woods, where they bunny-hopped over
a curb, through the intersection where they looked both
ways before crossing, under the streetlight, and into
the foyer of a home, where they shuffled out of dirty
sneakers, where they left their sneakers there and just
ran to find their parents and wanted to hug them, their
parents, because the kids were happy to be home, to
be safe, to be alive, and to not be like Tammy, the girl
who ran away from home because nobody liked her
because she liked her Tamagotchi too much because she
sat at the lunch table with her handheld best friend and
chatted quietly, almost in silence, and that those kids
who shouted words that stuck and pointed with fingers
that bruised, and that those kids were the ones who told
Tammy and Tammy's Tamagotchi to run away into the
New Jersey Pine Barrens every day as if some repetitive
saying, as if *just run away, Tammy* became Tammy's
name, and that Tammy Tamagotchi was synonymous
with Run-Away Tammy, and so Tammy ran away one
day; she brought her colorful backpack, the only thing
they found, and Tammy Tamagotchi became just a story,
a cautionary one, and her body sunk somewhere in the
ground, the sedimentary ground, that held rocks, and
dirt, and bones.

INHERITANCE

Ellen Birkett Morris

S ome people are born to sin; others inherit it. I didn't
know which of these I was until I crossed paths with
the Cabots.

The room smelled of lemons and vinegar. Alma
Cabot lay stiff across her cherry Duncan Phyfe table.
A tall woman, her legs almost reached the end of the
table. Her face was slack where it was usually stern, but
still, there was no trace of softness.

The table had a high shine. Our house didn't have
a mirror. When I looked down, my reflection startled
me. My hair hung in wild tendrils around my face. My
eyes were hard. I'd been sitting with the dead woman
for fifteen minutes according to the grandfather clock
in the corner.

Mrs. Cabot wore her best dress, purple brocade with
pearl buttons, and matching earrings. I was sure her
son Daniel would relieve her of these before her body
went into the ground. I heard pearls come from a grain
of sand that irritated the oyster. I wasn't surprised that
this was Mrs. Cabot's jewelry of choice.

Though she had absented her body, I half expected
Mrs. Cabot to pop up and start talking about the fine
wood finish, turned edges, and four-legged base of the
table. She loved ownership and often spoke about the

"fine pieces" her grandmother had brought over from England. She told these stories to anyone who would listen, including my mama, who spent years mopping the Cabots' floors and cooking their dinners—and then went home to a bed of straw ticking. If I had been my mother, I would have spit in the Cabots' food—or worse, but my mother played by the rules, ones that were set and broken by the Cabots. Because the Cabots had money, nobody said a thing. Mama believed in God's final judgment, but I wasn't sure it was wise to leave it up to Him, what with His reputation for mercy and all.

Mrs. Cabot would have squirmed at the thought of being laid out on her elegant table, though that was the custom around these parts. I wouldn't be seated at this table if she hadn't passed.

I was here for one reason, to take away her sins. My granny had been a sin eater, as her granny was before her, a custom from England that came with her across the ocean along with the family's meager belongings. Part of me thought the ritual was foolishness, though I never said so. The other part of me feared it was real and wondered about the weight of my granny's soul.

Before she died, Granny wrapped up her black cloak and left instructions with Mama that it was to be passed on to me. I liked to believe she thought I was tough enough to handle the job and smart enough not to take it too seriously. Either way, I'd been bearing the sins of the Cabots for a while now.

I was born on the wrong side of the river, in the elbow, a patch of land by the bend, prone to flooding. It was the kind of place people with no sense, or no money, lived. It took my family several generations before Daddy finally built the house up off the ground. So then, when it rained, we were on a dirtier version of Noah's ark, one with nearly as many inhabitants (Mama, Daddy, me, the twins, four feral cats, three dogs, a chicken, and two songbirds). With less food, of course.

Daniel Cabot had crossed the creek to fetch me that morning. It wasn't his first visit. That one was shortly after I turned sixteen, the summer that it flooded and our crops washed out. We almost starved that summer. Daddy let Daniel in and sent him to my room. I didn't know what was happening, but Daddy stood in my doorway and told me to make Daniel welcome; then he closed the door. Daniel stood still, looking at me. I saw his lust, but also a look like he was judging cattle. For all his looking, I don't think he saw me at all. Then he lifted my gown over my head and carried me to the bed.

He was his mother's son, greedy and prideful. He panted as he took me from behind. I stared at the water stain on the wall. It was big and yellowed with ragged brown edges in the shape of a dog. When I was little, I pretended it was real and called it Yeller, which always made my mama laugh. While Daniel labored, I imagined running through a wide field with Yeller, someplace far away from the elbow.

Daniel pressed his finger against my teeth until I figured I was meant to suck on it, which I did, though I fantasized about biting it off and feeding it to Yeller. At first, I gagged, but then I pretended it was a piece of ice melting in my mouth until it disappeared into nothing.

The Cabots owned the coal mine, but Daniel's finger was as soft as a baby's, unstained by labor. The nail was clean, though raggedy from his chewing it. He smelled of expensive soap, a sharp citrus smell that would come to signal danger to me. I said nothing while he spent his energy on me. I barely moved, hoping he'd get bored and move on. That night, and every visit after, he left fifty cents on my dresser. I never touched the money, but it always disappeared.

I was proud of myself for not crying out that night— or the many nights after. He would have wanted me to whimper and moan. But I didn't want to wake the little ones and stain their first memories with sounds of suffering. When he left, I rinsed my mouth at the washbasin and ran wet rags across my thighs. The rags came back bloody. The next morning Mama washed the stains from my sheets without a word.

This morning, Daniel had stood in the doorway and said, "Mother's dead. The corpse cakes are in the oven, and we need you down at the house."

I dressed quickly in my cloak and took a fine linen handkerchief from Mama's drawer. When we got to the house, I placed the handkerchief on the doorstep. I would retrieve it and the money when my work was done.

Daniel had pushed me roughly in the direction of the dining room and left me alone with her, while he went to fetch his brother. I knew Abraham by reputation only. He had been away at school and then opened a law practice in Charleston.

I walked around the room, running my finger across the scrolls and leaves of the carved sideboard. I slid open a drawer to find linens embroidered with sprigs of lavender. A small sachet of lavender was in the corner of the drawer. I held it to my nose; the sweet, fresh scent reminded me that just outside these walls, the fields were bursting with life. I went back to the table and sat across from Mrs. Cabot, where I could see her face as it slowly turned to stone.

I had been a sin eater before, but that family was strangers to me, folks who had come into the mining camps from Pittsburgh and lost their daughter to the flu. I wondered how much sin she could have accumulated in her five years, not much I would reckon, but the family was superstitious and wanted to send her off to the afterlife with a clean slate. The girl had taken up only a small portion of the table. A corpse cake had laid on her small chest. I said the words, and the mother handed me the cake. The cake had raisins and currants inside and crumbled in my mouth. The family watched as I ate every crumb. When I got outside, two dollars sat on my handkerchief.

I waited until I got into the woods to stick my finger down my throat. A volcano of sweet cake and fruit left a mess in the grass. It was no time at all before the bees came buzzing around it. I figured I'd only taken in a little of the sin, nothing mortal, nothing that would keep me from heaven.

I was jumpy today, my stomach a strange mix of nausea and hunger. I was used to hunger, but the nausea was a more recent development. I had been waking up with my stomach roiling around. I kept a few peppermint leaves inside my pillow and chewed on them when things got bad.

I ran my hand around the smooth edge of the table. I could do anything now—carve my initials into the underside with my pocket knife, slide the silver sugar shell into my pocket, take a piece of the old woman's hair for some kind of hex. But instead, I touched my stomach and whispered in the dead woman's ear, "I'm carrying your grandchild."

Nobody could tell yet. The small swell in my belly was hidden by my dress. But my state would reveal itself soon—and there would be hell to pay. I looked out the window at the tall oak standing in front of the house. It was a huge old tree with a gnarled trunk. The thick branches came out like tentacles spreading toward the sun, taking up space against the sky. I saw a strong, low branch, a perfect place to perch and watch the world, and I took in the sturdy branches just beyond, footholds to the sky. My son would never play there.

I heard the back door close, and I sat back quickly and raised the hood of my cloak to obscure my face. Daniel pushed the door open, a plate of cakes in his hand, and he held the door for another man. Abraham was tall and resembled Daniel around the nose and forehead, but he had much kinder eyes.

He reached his hand out toward me.

"Don't bother," said Daniel.

The man raised his eyebrows. I held back a smile.

Abraham looked at his mother. "She's not here. There is no trace of her," he said quietly.

"Only death could still the likes of her," said Daniel.

"What is this?" asked Abraham, nodding at me.

"A local burial custom of the rabble, some malarkey about eating the sins of the deceased. Mother insisted we do it if she should die."

If she should die! Did the Cabots think immortality was theirs for the taking, like everything else?

Daniel laid the plate of cakes on his mother's still chest.

The cakes were round and small and black around the edges.

The brothers looked at me expectantly.

I picked up a cake and held it to my mouth. When my teeth bit down, I felt like a vulture feasting on the entrails of some small, soft animal that had gotten in the way, but I knew I was that small, soft animal and Daniel wouldn't quit visiting me at night until nothing was left of me but a crimson stain on the floor. I chewed and swallowed, felt the hard cake scrape down my throat.

I heard myself speak, though in my mind, I was far above the house, circling, waiting for my chance to pounce. My voice was loud and strong.

"I pledge my soul for your sins and ask that God Almighty remove those sins from you and place them up on me, and I eat this food to show that I have taken your sins upon me. If I lie, may God strike me dead."

I looked at the brothers, whose eyes were closed. It was done. I walked to the door. I could see the coins shining on my handkerchief. I bent down to scoop them up. I felt a presence behind me. Abraham stepped forward and pressed five dollars into my hands. I looked him in the face, wondering if my son would look like him.

It was enough money for the train east. I could be alone with my sins. I'd find a place somewhere, get a dog, and take in sewing. I would be free. My son would live unencumbered by legacy, free in a way I could only imagine. I walked quickly through the woods, stopping only to put my finger down my throat.

I rushed home and began to pack. I took my two dresses, crochet hook, and knitting needles and the skein of yarn I had been saving to make mittens for the twins. I stopped to touch the stain on the wall, which, in the light of day, looked like nothing but a dirty spot.

Mama stood in my doorway. "Don't," she said.

"I've got to." My hand wandered to the five dollars folded in my pockets. I looked into her face and noticed the lines worn into its surface, the hollows of her checks.

"We'll starve."

If I stayed, I would become her, more indebted to the Cabots with each passing day for whatever table scraps they decided to throw my way, like a dog—worse than a dog, since I was more than my appetites.

I pushed past her and ran out the door. I ran all the way to town and bought a ticket to Richmond. I barely had time to sit down before the train pulled up. It was my first time on a train. The seats were covered in leather, and the interior was trimmed in wood. I knew I stood out in my simple dress and mended shawl. I took a seat near the door. It wasn't long before the rocking of the cars lulled me to sleep. It was a dreamless sleep, not like my dreams at home, where I was forever trying to escape from some unknown pursuer.

I woke up as a man made his way down the aisle with a trolley that carried a teakettle and cake. "Refreshment, miss?"

I had a cup of tea with cream and sugar. I sipped it slowly. When I got settled, this would be my new ritual—a cup of tea in the quiet of the afternoon while the baby slept. Prince, West Virginia, its hunger and fear, would be far behind me.

I got off in Charleston, searching for the way to my connecting train. I had only taken a few steps when I felt a hand grab my arm and smelled the citrus scent of Daniel's soap.

I pulled my arm away, and he reached forward and held me tight. I struggled to break free and stomped on his foot.

He pushed my face close to his and spoke through gritted teeth. "I'll tell them you robbed me. They'll find the rest of Abe's money on you, and you will go to jail."

I stopped struggling and looked beyond Daniel to see my train pulling out of the station. "How did you find me?"

"Your mother told me you were running away. I knew you wouldn't get far on foot. I saw Abe hand you the money and figured you'd go to the train station."

My mother was foolish enough to see the Cabots as benefactors.

*

I was silent on the train ride home. Daniel stared at me, his mouth twisted into a smirk. "You're hardly worth the trouble. Your bloom is fading, and you're getting fat."

He was ignorant as well as mean. I had nothing now, no family, no allies, just the hint of possibility in my womb that I was sure Daniel would take from me the minute he was born.

When I got home, I hugged Mama and smiled at Daddy. Let them think I was content to stay. I waited until the middle of the night to leave my bed and put on my black cloak. I touched the wall to say goodbye to Yeller.

*

The rope hung on a nail on the wall of the barn. It wasn't heavy. I made it to the oak before the moon had emerged from the clouds.

I climbed to a high branch. The face of the Cabots' house was silent. How surprised Daniel would be in the morning. How quickly word would spread among the neighbors. I'd seen my father hang pigs upside down to drain the blood plenty of times. I secured the rope, fashioned a noose, and placed it around my neck.

I imagined my body swaying in the wind, a spectral figure in my dark cloak. The bees would still buzz, the river would flood, girls would get visited in the night, and the Cabots would sit counting their money, polishing their silver, with no idea of what had been taken from them. I let myself fall.

FEEDING TIME

Jen Soong

The moon is half-full and you are packing the only suitcase you own. Well, it's your ma's but she doesn't know. The exterior is robin's-egg blue with a hard shell and hairline white cracks zigzagging like lightning. Your neck cranes toward the soft blue interior pockets and you inhale cedar mothballs.

You remember near the end, Ama spent days in the humid bedroom with lemon walls you shared, barely lifting her eyelids. Her hollow cheeks warned of death. Sometimes her arms shot up skyward and she shouted at you, "Go!" in the gruff baritone of a five-star general.

Where would you go, you wondered. You only knew the mildewed walls of your railroad apartment, where you, eldest of three girls, spooned out ginger rice porridge to squabbling mouths while Ma was hunched over a Singer hand crank at Old Tailor's shop with her weary eyes and prayerful hands. You only knew a wandering dirt path from your squat two-story building to a one-room school to a makeshift hospital where your father doled out medicinal tinctures and hope to children who lost their toes, fingers, even eyeballs, in a forgotten war's minefield. You only knew neglected contours of the island you called home. You only knew a decaying cemetery where bones were buried without headstones.

You imagined a life where you didn't answer to anyone's prayers—not your mother's, not your grandmother's, not your ancestors'—by marrying into riches with gold and jade bowls and plum-cheeked babies. But you never dared to map an escape route. Your mother sinks day by day deeper into her grief-ridden husk, shoulders collapsing into dust. Disappearing.

You can't remember the last time she sang. Her voice, soft and cooing, used to fill your heart with music. Sunlight danced on windowsills. Your little hands waved to passing skylarks. Laughter and song once overfilled your home. You plucked purple blazing stars for her black hair flowing past her waist, and she lifted you toward the clouds. You flew with the larks.

Then, the bombs fell from the sky and air raid sirens replaced her singing.

Moonlight illuminates a gold locket Ama gave you on your tenth birthday. You remember how she looked at you, her dark eyes narrowing to crescents, and you squirmed under her gaze. Promise you will take it when you go, she said. Promise.

You finger the curves of the locket, wishing you had listened to her old woman ramblings, taking her growls more gravely. It was only after she died on your seventeenth birthday that you heard a chorus of loud voices. It was as if she had passed them to you when she crossed over the riverbed. They chanted, demanded, banged on buffalo-hide drums, willing you to *go, go, go*. You tried to block out their angry voices by shouting back and wailing *no, no, no*. Alas, it was no use.

The dead live inside your chest walls now.

You pack everything you stole from Neighbor Li's kitchen (you waited until she went to the temple) in red paper: mandarins, pomegranates, shrimp balls, oyster mushrooms, longevity noodles, sweet rice cakes, and whole carp with eyeballs for good luck. An intoxicating feast. You kiss the suitcase closed. Ma would not approve. You cannot save everyone.

At the end of the month, a hungry ghost moon will rise. Their cries shake and shatter your eardrums. Their stubborn knocking pounds against your chest. *You must go.* Your time, Ama commands. You must make your way to the moon. You must feed our hungry ghosts.

ESCAPE

DeMisty D. Bellinger

Monisha was famous for not crawling. At ten years old, she read all of Shakespeare's sonnets and his comedies, writing a couple of papers, and publishing them in two separate peer-reviewed journals with minimum edits. Her counterparts in the public education and job centers took quickly to a trade that they could fulfill until the ultra rich figured out a way to automate those jobs, too. But Monisha excelled in calculus, physics, English, and biochemistry. It was very likely that she would leave. Eyes were already on her, and conversations were already happening. Her parents stared at her when they thought she wasn't noticing.

She noticed.

Last week, she told her parents that she will be a woman. "It isn't yet practical, but it's how I feel inside."

Her parents didn't question her, didn't discourage her from her choice or encourage her to, at the very least, go with nonbinary until she was old enough to know for sure, because they knew Monisha was wise enough to know by now. She walked at eight months. Never crawled.

Tatum was overly proud of their daughter. He was sure her wit and studiousness were products of a formula he had concocted for her before she could eat solid food.

He and his wife grew up as the American dream drew its last breaths, but Tatum was sure it was not dead quite yet. Even now, there was a chance for social and economic mobility. Yes, it didn't matter if you went to college or grad school; those chances gave you a life that was good enough, but no one moved from the middle class to the ultra rich unless they had real talents.

Monisha, Tatum was certain, had real talents.

Daysha's heart would beat when she'd catch herself wishing that Monisha would leave already. Something about the child made her apprehensive. Something about her daughter made Daysha realize that Tatum was lacking. She looked at Monisha and saw her husband, saw an obtuse, helpless hope in spite of the reality laid out before them. If Monisha did get to leave, get to go to an actual school and study actual academics, to what end would it be? It'd be for the ultra rich to save the lives of those who destroyed the middle and working classes' lives. Daysha knew: the very wealthy had clear skies and clean air uninhibited by UV-protected shields. Daysha knew that the ultra rich could actually go outside.

When Daysha was Monisha's age, she used to sit outside her mother's house on the stoop, watching the other girls play jump rope and waiting her turn. She closed her eyes and felt the summer sun warming her face, turning her already brown skin browner with just the tinge of red as deep as a burgundy. A summer glow. She could hear the cicada and grasshopper songs, along with the piercing cry of the blue jays and rude caws of the crows that dominated her neighborhood. She could remember the maple leaves shading her haphazardly, letting spots of sun rays through, and lone leaves shaking on their own, as if they were moved to dance.

Leaves.

Outside now, no more lawns, and all the trees were dwarfed and utilitarian. Outside, no more simplicity of sitting in the sun, lest you wanted to get basal cell or squama cell carcinoma, or melanoma, or worse, first-degree burns.

Leaves.

Again, Daysha's heart rate sped up, the word delicious in her mind, but not for Monisha. It was delicious to her. Get up and go, Daysha, she thought.

But then what? And to where?

Tatum, oblivious to all around him and so full of helpless hope, picks Monisha up in his arms and spins with her. The child giggles. They are in their living room of their apartment pod, well taken care of. They have enough. And Daysha, too aware of what is happening, sits on the sofa and smiles blankly at the two of them. When Tatum sets Monisha back down on her feet, the girl looks at her mother. Daysha's breath catches somewhere in her esophagus with fear of being found out, but she sees it in Monisha's eyes, too, Monisha who famously never crawled, the desire of escape to somewhere else.

UNDERWATER EVEN BELLS SOUND LIKE BODIES

Chloe N. Clark

V iv discovered she could separate her arm from her body one morning while making pancakes. She remembered to leave clumps in the batter, ladled the batter onto the hot griddle with practiced care. Her left arm, doing nothing useful in the operation, began to inch away from her. Starting at her shoulder blade, it popped itself loose with a sound like an air-filled paper bag being smacked between two hands. Viv stared at her arm as it crawled across the countertop.

She didn't swear or scream, because she wasn't the type. Even as a little child, she'd once fallen into a rattlesnake nest and had lain so still, so fascinated by the mess of scaled and gently hissing bodies around her, that nothing bad had happened. Her mother had wondered if it was a miracle. Her father had called it luck. Her grandmother said, "But, well, hasn't this one got a little witch in her."

Viv's arm stopped crawling when it reached the cookie jar. It was caught in a rousing attempt to open the jar by itself. "What the hell will you do with a cookie?" Viv asked, startled to realize that she was talking to her arm as if it were not a part of her. She corrected, "What the hell will I do with a cookie?"

The arm gave up, slinking back to her, knuckles drooping down in defeat. With one athletic leap, it reattached to her body. Viv finished making the pancakes and began to wonder how long her arm had been able to do such a thing. Did it leave her while she was sleeping? Go for moonlit walks or paint pictures of the ocean? Someplace she had never seen in person but dreamed of so often that sometimes she woke up with her hair soaking wet.

She ate pancakes at her desk. Her job was writing copy for travel sites. She wrote about places she'd never been. She imagined the trees south of her, which hung thick with moss. She daydreamed beaches onto the screen. When people read her copy, they could feel the heat, the wind, the waves. They smelled food with spices that had never before lingered on their tongues. They heard voices, voices, voices. As she typed, she felt another pop. It was her leg this time, lifting itself away from the crease where thigh met pelvis. It stepped away from her, wobbly as a toddler on its own. She rooted for it to find its balance. Cheering when it bent at the knee to give itself a little less weight at the top. Her single leg hopped over to the window, leaned against the wall.

It didn't reattach until she was almost done with work and needed to pee. She asked politely, and it rejoined her. She ate dinner alone that night, just her and her body. Her wife on another long shift, texting her she missed her, texting her that every patient she saw was worse than the last. She was a paramedic, but in these times might as well have been an ice cream truck driver. She brought solace but nothing else.

Viv took a bath, smoothed her hands over her skin. As a child, she'd never liked Barbies but had enjoyed disassembling them. She'd pop off an arm, a head, slice open a leg to see the frame that let their joints move. She was convinced that her skeleton looked the same. One day, she'd felt bad, patched the Barbies up with bandages and tape and glue. She'd made a raft of twigs and sent them down the stream in the forest behind her house. She wanted them to be free of her.

When her wife got home, Viv was already in bed, falling into dreams. Her wife molded her body to hers, warm and soft as the first day they met. They'd danced at their wedding, though Viv had no rhythm. But her wife had said, take some of mine, and suddenly Viv's feet had moved like a symphony.

"My body wants to leave me," Viv mumbled from her sleep.

"But you're the best place to be," her wife said.

In the morning, Viv went to the garden. She let her arms and legs step away from her. She lay on the ground, waiting. Her arm returned first, muddy from the banks of the river. Then a leg, sticky with sweat from learning how to run by itself. Then the next arm. The next leg. Viv sat up, watched the sky.

She texted her wife, "Let's go to the sea. Can we go to the sea?"

Her wife responded. "Yes, of course, yes."

Viv wondered how far out she could swim. If her legs and her arms might carry her all the way to the horizon.

FENIX PEPPER

Matt Barrett

I taught my brother Fenix to take his fears and worries and scream them in a Mason jar so when he shut the lid, they had to fight until all that remained was a calming whoosh of air inside a glass. It didn't matter if you screamed your hate and anger or read Shakespeare's plays, when you went back to open that jar, it was the same quiet sound inside.

When the state came to pick us up, Fenix chose to run. He said they couldn't take us from our daddy, even though they could. They could do anything. All they had to do was grab us by the wrist and shove us in the back of their slick black car. We could scream so our angry words traveled in the backseat with us, on our way to some big yellow room with big yellow bunks and thin yellow sheets for all the others who were taken from their daddies and mommies to hide beneath when they told us in the dark to shut our eyes.

But not that day in June. Not that day when the car pulled up and we were busy shouting the things we wanted to yell at the world inside our Mason jars. Not when the men in sunglasses and big black suits asked, "Are you the Pepper boys?"

Yeah, we were the Pepper boys. The boys who'd heard the jokes already—so come on, throw one at us, see how they make us feel. *Your daddy a doctor or some-thing? Ha-ha. Yo, Jalapeño!* Or tell us our favorite: *Did Peter Piper pick the peck of you?*

Fenix Pepper, man. Named Fenix because our mother didn't know how to spell Phoenix. Named Fenix for the city, not the bird, Fenix because our names had to have an x somewhere, Xavier and Knox, Alexander and Dax. We were the X Kids, the former kids, who had to grow up too fast.

When Fenix took off running, the men followed but not for long. He ran faster than any man in a suit could ever dream. When he reached the woods, he called, "I'm sorry Dax, I'm sorry Knox!" Only his voice was so scared and thin, it didn't sound like words until we asked ourselves in the back of that slick black car what he might have said. *Sorry*, we agreed. We wished we could have told him, "It's okay." We wished we could have yelled, "Just keep running, Fenix!" We wished we could have seen ourselves in those men's sunglasses, our skinny frames and dirty mouths, and said, "You're gonna have to catch us, too." But we'd told ourselves the lie that they could do anything. We told ourselves no matter how far we ran, they'd catch up to us someday. We told ourselves those men would always win.

But not Fenix. Only Fenix saw himself staring back in those men's glasses and noticed how wide the world really was. Maybe he saw the woods back there and a way out—maybe it was all right there, in those shiny black frames we were too scared to face ourselves.

We never looked. We told ourselves no good could come of raising our heads, just stare at the ground and say *yes sir*. But I remember when Fenix held the Mason jar to his ear, he said he heard his thoughts even louder than before. All his fears, all those worries—they started barking at him, he said. Not that quiet whoosh. Not that calming sound we aimed for, not the peace we thought sounded like lights out. Not the *Shh, go to bed now*, not the *Please don't say another word*. Not *Did anyone ask you to speak, Mr. Pepper Boy?* He heard *Run*. He heard *Go*. And when he heard it, he listened, his ear pressed so tight to the lip of his jar, the voice inside was louder than anyone's who told him to stop.

THE EASTER BUNNY AND THE THEORETICAL MASS

Caroline Macon Fleischer

A spick-and-span gold handlebar descended the epic staircase at Hilltop University. The steps alternated ruby and gold, gold and ruby, the spirit colors of the prestigious school. Fresh mulch and thoughtfully spaced tulips surrounded the stairway's entrance. Even the flowers looked sprightly in ruby and gold—a cheerleading squad to welcome me in.

My fingers were as stiff as freezer pops. For my commute, I'd walked, then taken a bus, then walked again. It was a chilly day in disguise with its orange morning rays of spring sunshine. I couldn't wait to settle in and get my costume on, certain the big paws would warm my hands right up. For five years, I'd played the Easter Bunny at the annual Hilltop Charity Carnival, and it had grown to be the main event of my life.

The extravaganza was a rare, special day that gave me a sense of belonging, worth, and escape. It didn't make me any money and since playing the Easter Bunny was an act of charity, the earnings included an unrivaled lesson in amour propre. The once-a-year shift added intention to my life as no other activity did—and I didn't even need to be a seasoned actor to play the part. All I had to do was arrive on time, with an open heart, put on my costume, and sit. Bunnies weren't expected to talk. We weren't Santa Clauses.

I wished I could volunteer every day.

The Hilltop Charity Carnival was a free-admission Easter event that was ostensibly open to everyone. Its marketed mission was to give a jolly experience to those who sometimes couldn't afford jolly experiences. But obviously, the underlying mission was to raise money. Upon entry, the richer folks could donate if they wanted through raffles, silent auctions, and pledges.

However, while scanning the crowd years prior, I'd noticed its demographic had missed the mark. The mob tended to only be the academic Hilltop crowd—old-money academic types and their intellectually-questionable-but-athletically-engineered heirs. The intended communities were never in the mix to enjoy the festivities. The bunny photos, beers, and Ferris wheel rides were all going to the rich and distinguished.

By the fifth year, I'd taken it as my duty to spread the word to the underserved. I'd handed out flyers at halfway houses, street corners, needle exchanges, and soup kitchens. I was comfortable in these spaces and had frequented them regularly in my past life. Then, in my new life as a more stable person, one who partook in charity not as a requirement to correct some wrong but as a philanthropic escape, I reasoned that my charity had better be authentic. If the underprivileged didn't arrive, all my efforts and convictions would have been for naught.

To kickstart the day, the volunteers had a mandatory informational session. Over Dunkin' Box O' Joes and too many boxes of glazed, we rounded up inside the university gym. In years prior, they'd had a full breakfast buffet and a DJ for us. Now their priorities had changed, but I couldn't blame them—the festival was growing and all for a noble cause. Ryan, who had cofounded the Hilltop Charity Carnival with his wife whose name I still didn't know, planted himself at a podium in the center of the basketball court like an evangelical pastor. We were his scattered congregation in the stands, mouth-breathing with lukewarm coffees and sticky, glazy palms.

"Thank you for joining us this morning," he said. "I welcome all your faces, both familiar and new. Elory," he said and looked at me, "welcome back for—how many years has it been?"

"Five," I said, proud. I could feel the other volunteers get jealous.

"Five. Wow," Ryan said and clapped once. The wife-founder smiled with a shallow puddle of a dimple and waved at me with one finger.

"I know many of you have been forced to volunteer because you've done wrong—according to our government or society or what-have-you—and you need to make it right. Maybe you're an addict, a criminal, or even just a traffic law violator. I don't know why you're here and I don't care. But I hope that once you've redeemed your wrong, you'll come back. Because like Elory here, I hope you'll become addicted to the rush of service. It's how I started, too. You won't believe it—I was in your place once. I once had to pick up trash on the side of a highway for a full *weekend* after I shoplifted a case of Michelob Ultra."

A few shifts and squeaks sounded from the stands. "Ha ha. I know you don't believe me. It was a different time," Ryan said. "Then once I got a hit of making others' lives better, I couldn't get enough."

His words resonated with me as a sermon would. I wasn't a criminal but a recovering alcoholic, and continued to deal with the urge to slam cold ones, or warm ones, or snacks of pills, as well as unrelenting depression. It was because of this unrelenting depression that I was asked to volunteer for the event in the first place. In my sober group five years prior, my sponsor Kelly noted, astutely, that I was numb and that nothing brought me joy.

When I couldn't decide on an action plan that would fix this observation, she decided for me. And she was right. For starters, charity mended a broken heart. I was reeling from a soul-crushing breakup. Volunteering gave my days on this planet more measurable goals, to report on time and perform my task, and get thanked. It gave me purpose; by fulfilling my duty as the Easter Bunny, I had an individual purpose that was separate from my substance abuse and old boyfriend and general mopery. And clinical gloom.

Before arriving at this solution, I'd gone on SSRIs, and they'd made me ill. Then I'd gone to a psychiatrist who did what psychiatrists should never do—put a recovering alcoholic on narcotics. I continued taking the narcotics but knew they were an incomplete plan of attack against the shadowy void of sadness. After a long and strenuous debacle of laying on my old boyfriend's front lawn and crying my eyes out, his new girlfriend came outside and put me in her car and drove me to a group therapy center. There, I tucked myself cozily beneath my brilliant sponsor Kelly's wing. Buried in her warm, feathery armpit, I made real progress.

Back in those days, I'd have to get signatures on tiny little yellow sheets of paper until my probation was up. But then Kelly killed herself, and no one checked my papers anymore. I hung them all on my refrigerator, so I could habitually feel proud about my progress, even when I sometimes lacked progress, which was all a part of recovery—as Kelly would say.

There in the gym, looking around the room at the other volunteers, I was curious about how many others in the room felt depressed. I supposed it was a high statistical percentage—at least eighty-four percent, a figure I made up to be high but not unrealistically high. Vacant eyes, septum piercings, and multicolored hair surrounded me, all normal indications that someone isn't doing well. My hair was just brown, and I didn't have any piercings, so people didn't pry as to how I was doing. My sadness manifested more in a way that was like, I didn't do laundry much or shower enough and all I did was call my old boyfriend over and over, even though he had my number blocked, so I could listen to the sound of his voice on his voicemail greeting.

I confess that every year when I registered to serve at the carnival, I wondered if he would attend. He was an adjunct professor there, so the chances were slim but not unheard of. I thought about looking at him from inside the big bunny mask. I thought about him sitting on one of my legs with his niece on my other leg, prompting her to smile for the camera with the Easter Bunny. I wanted to see him so desperately, even knowing he didn't want to see me back. His new girlfriend was a nice young woman who was fresh-faced and sober, according to her straight-core aura, and smelled like Dove soap and turned her ear into me when I talked to her which allowed me to feel heard. She'd been so nice to me the two times I met her briefly, which only got me feeling worse.

After the introduction, the rest of the orientation was a blur. I didn't listen because I already knew the rules and regulations. As I thought of my old boyfriend and his great new girl, I melted behind a thin glass of tears. This happened a lot, but I could cry so subtly people didn't even notice. My body didn't shake. It was a quiet, hesitant cry, undetectable by anyone but me. It would be even less noticeable when I put on the Easter Bunny mask. In there, I could shake and heave if I wanted, my sobs echoing in the darkness.

After his speech, Ryan released us to visit the wife and receive our assignments and instructions. Since I knew where to go and what to do, I slipped past without a word. Affirming me as an old pro, she gave me a gimmicky salute. I headed to the women's locker room where the costume waited for me in a janitorial closet. I was extra small so when they'd hired me, they had to place a special junior order. Even though I was the only one who wore it, I liked leaving it in the possession of Hilltop Charity until the next season, knowing it was there year-round waiting for my selfless act of service.

It was also a test of patience for me. Going home without it every year made the bus ride feel long and dreary. Sometimes I wished I could hold its head in my lap while I looked out the window, tracing its cute pout and whiskers with my fingers, wishing I could feel its warm breath on me like a real pet. I knew lots of people hated mascots or felt fear or discomfort, but I found them comforting, their big circular eyes glistening with peaceful energy. Without my costume, I felt incomplete.

But I knew I needed to actively challenge that feeling or there would be no hope for me to be a real person. Like all the other real people. I liked how mascots were silent and still until someone was inside them. Before the event, I wanted to drink. And I didn't want to drink. And I wanted to drink.

In a lifelong study conducted privately by me, I concluded that normal people who had only used substances occasionally did not understand this gleeful blip that substances are meant to ignite and imagined this paradise as hell. It's like the hottest bubbles floating in the lava lamp, and I wanted to be in the hottest place— transcending all those natural and known geometrical shapes and becoming a new, unique, languid blob.

Usually, I stayed safe, with a single Miller Lite or a glass of Chardonnay. But that day, I pined for something more for my special retreat. I still lived with my mother and her drink in stock was tequila. Like many mothers, she didn't take my drinking problem seriously but took her own seriously: i.e., martyr mom; i.e., *every one of your bad traits is my fault, but not enough of my fault for me to change*; i.e., *my faults make me sad*; i.e., *but sadness is not actionable*, i.e., hopelessness.

The spring cold front had me feeling extra, super down. Tequila felt springy. So, I'd packed a little Thermos with a little tequila, squeezed a little lime juice into the bottom with a little splash of cold lemonade, and shook.

There in the locker room before the costume, I sipped the homemade margarita and tried to reach that heavenly space. One sip became another which became a third which became a fourth. After four big gulps, I stopped. It was time to put on the costume and remember what it felt like to not be seen as me anymore.

The thing looked so happy hanging before me, joking with me, like he wanted a pull of the bottle, too. I pulled it off the hanger, loopy, and stumbled into the thing. In this iteration of my cross-faded promised land, my old boyfriend's voicemail played on repeat in my head. It was nostalgic—the sound was fuzzy like the radio speakers at the public pool. He was saying hello and that he would call me back later. I loved the way his sound moved from his chest to his mouth to the phone receiver to me. I loved him so much. I missed him every minute.

Once in costume, wobbling, I faced the mirror. I wish I looked so kind every day, so cheerful, so simple. This was the face of kindness, the face that I lacked. The eyes twinkled like fairy lights and the cheeks were as funny as fun. Seeing myself in this jim-dandy state made me sick over who I truly was—addicted, empty, a dripping cavern of broken yearning.

I could have gotten a bunny as a pet—but I didn't even think I could manage that. I didn't think I could do anything others did. I didn't know how. I wished I could just be a bunny—surely, they didn't endure the suffering of humankind. Surely, they needed food, warmth, and shelter and not much else. All I wanted was to reduce myself to that level rather than live in this misery I'd created and become trapped in. I needed to get out.

I needed it so much that I prayed for it. I said, "God, please, I am calling out to you as a nasty, busted, theoretical mass of a person. I had potential at birth, but since, I have rotted. You care for rotting people, don't you? Do you love us? Doesn't the big old Good Book say that in so many words? If it's true, I beg you. Please never make me endure the suffering of human girlhood ever again. Either kill me now or make me a bunny. I don't want this anymore. Please." With that, I stretched my arms above my head and tugged at the mascot head.

It wouldn't wiggle. I heaved.

I tried to pull it, but my skin hurt. My tiny body in the extra small costume seemed to grow and stick to the insides of the animal's skin like superglue. But rather than fear, I felt relief. God loved me When I looked into my new eyes in the mirror, I relaxed, soaking in gratitude, thankful that I'd never be a girl again or have to mess with any of the things that came with it.

That year, my old boyfriend did go to the carnival. He brought his new girl. He brought his giggling niece. She sat on my lap while the happy couple leaned in around either side of me, grinning for the flash. They didn't know who I was. I was pleased as punch. Then I took the next bus out to the nearest meadow to lie down in some shrubbery.

POCKETED

Sarah Fawn Montgomery

Polly is as small as your fingernail, but shiny and clean, not like your ragged half-moons, the ones you use to dig in the sandbox as though you are trying to escape, drag across your thighs to leave pale tracks, skin turned to dust as if to confirm how easily you can be reduced to nothing.

Polly wears a red headband around her blond curls, and you try in the bathroom mirror, balancing on the sink, to see yourself as if for the first time, gangly gap-toothed girl playing dress-up behind the toothpaste spray. When you lean forward to magnify your desperation, smell old food and sharp sting of Listerine.

Polly keeps a dog and a cat at her country cottage, a basket of kittens and a koi pond at her parade village. She looks after animals in her veterinary hospital. They smile even though you know this isn't possible. Dogs like yours jump the metal fence to run away, choke themselves hoarse trying to escape the chain. Your haunchy cat slinks the yard like a premonition.

You find disemboweled mice on the porch—blue and yellow gut sacks, heads held on by strings. You feel that way sometimes, like you would drift away if not for the tether of your spine. Severed hands and feet—tiny as your plastic Polly Pocket, a dollhouse that fits in you palm—try to scurry off the cement.

The cat loves Mommy best, brings her baby bunnies, wild-eyed and frozen. Mommy pries them from the cat's jaws, walks into the field across the street—dead with weed and dust, broken bottles and cigarette butts—to set them free.

Polly hosts sleepovers in her pastel living room, volleyball parties on her private beach. Polly has a secret garden, a magic jungle.

No one comes to your sleepovers because last week a bar fight left a man dead on Main Street. Because the house by the riverbed pulses meth smoke like rotten eggs. Because the rusted-out cars look like piles of bones. Because your parents fight so big and loud that you hide beneath your bed. Because you said out loud that your swollen eyes make your lashes look like spiders when you look to the sky.

Make a fake beach in your sandbox, pretend stranded and please help. Struggle for air like drowning so good that sometimes you for real can't breathe. Make a garden of dirt clods. Hang ribbon from the doorway of your playhouse, pretend Polly walking through jungle vines. Pretend so good you imagine them snakes like in your nightmares, all that thrash and gnash in the sheets trying to escape.

Polly's houses are plastic compacts shaped like a star, like a flower, soapsuds, a seashell. Polly fits inside anything beautiful. Polly makes anyplace a home. She even fits in your hand-me-down pocket, the one sagging at the corner where you bury your hand, your head. Where you try to climb inside.

Your house is getting bigger, like the shouting is pushing out the walls. Or maybe it's you getting smaller. Your clothes don't fit right, your bed's too wide. You must be imagining it, you think, even the thought too big for your skull, floating out and above your head. Your plastic bank, the empty girl you drop pennies into, is nearly your height now, and even the ballerina in your music box twirls large in front of your face.

Your feelings don't fit, like how a feel slips out your mouth and you say *stop* or *no*, your heart struggling inside your small, aorta pumping at your throat.

Polly's smile has worn off under your frantic fingers, but you draw one in red pen to match your own wavering line.

There are rattlesnakes in the yard, black widows in the eaves, sex predators down the street. Your principal ran away with your classmate. He was nice, covered your small hand with his largeness.

Your neighbor spies from his second-story window, whispers through the knothole in the fence that he watches you undress. Your other neighbor never sleeps, mutters on the porch about ghosts, pops his head over the fence when you take out the garbage to say it's the end of the world.

You crouch when you undress, try to hide from the man peering inside your pastel room. You hold plastic still.

You crouch smaller when you take out the garbage, bones splitting the bag, revealing the gnaw where someone sucked out the sweet marrow. Whiskey bottles bang your shins, leave them mottled purple and blue like Mommy's arms, the place around her eye.

You crouch smallest to escape the neighbor's arms reaching over the fence towards you, pleading, "Let me save you, girl."

Daddy watches boxing on TV while you play Polly in her tiny jewel house. The sound of fist on flesh is familiar, and does anyone notice how you shrink? Now you fit in the suitcase Mommy is rolling to the front door, the bruise across her back, the box of Band-Aids she keeps beneath the sink.

Polly grows and grows or you shrink and shrink and now she is bigger than your nail, your finger, your whole clenched hand, tendons tight against the cage of your skin.

One man punches another, teeth down the throat. Blood spatters across the screen like stars, like the twinkle lights in Polly's enchanted garden.

You climb inside Polly's house when Mommy closes the door. The tiny dog and cat meet you. The koi fish leap from the pond in greeting. You smell the sterile safe of plastic. You walk the path, sit quiet on the bench. Everywhere is green. There are no neighbors. You can't even find Polly.

Inside the house, the bed is big enough for one. The couch too. There is no fighting on the TV. There is no toothpaste on the bathroom mirror when you check your Polly hair, Polly smile.

Grab the lid, snap the compact closed. Now you are hidden, safe in this brittle plastic heart.

WHEN THEY COME FOR THE WOLVES

Anna Gates Ha

I t's illegal now to kill the wolves, but the men say they'll do it anyway. Recovery my ass, they say. They gather their guns and ghillie suits and stand in front of the hearth.

A girl sits under the table, watching the men in their suits meant to mimic foliage and moss, and thinks of shaggy Muppets. She giggles.

No place for a little girl, her father says as he carries her up to her room, his entire form meant to disappear into the woods, but the fabric feels nothing like the forest, and the girl knows the wolves will not be fooled.

To find a wolf, you need to become the wolf. (Was it her mother who told her this? Whispered it as the window fogged with their breath? Was it before she died? Was it a fairy tale? The girl is always mixing up the two. Or so her father says.)

It's then that the word comes to her mind—a word her father calls the wolves, a word he used to call her mother. And with that word, with the violence laced on her father's tongue when he says it, comes a decision: she needs to leave before he can call her one, too.

She steals a wolf pelt from her father's bed, wraps it around her shoulders, tosses her hair, growls. She ties it around her neck and crawls along the floorboards, sniffing everything, rubbing her body on the edge of the bed, the table, coating everything with her scent. She crawls down the concrete steps to the basement, which is filled with coolers filled with frozen meat. She wraps a salmon the length of her arm in newspaper, zips it in her backpack (the pink one with an ice cream cone on it) and sets off into the forest to save a wolf.

The night is still and bright. She shivers under the moon. Follows prints in the snow, just like her mother taught her.

The wolf is not as she expects it. She finds it sitting on an exposed birch root, watching her.

The girl feels her heartbeat, then, feels how loud and out of place it is. Fragile little thing in the forest. The wolf's eyes are yellow, more yellow than the sun. She remembers now that she has not brought a weapon. Even her nails are chewed to the pink. The girl and the wolf stare at each other until the girl slips off her backpack and kneels in the snow. The wolf rises onto its feet, a puff of white steam leaves its muzzle. The girl throws the salmon as far as she can, but she is so little, her arms thin from being inside all winter, and it falls without a sound in the powdery snow a few feet in front of her. The wolf sniffs the air and stalks toward the salmon. Hesitant, at first, and then ravenous. It eats it there, in front of the girl, its teeth shredding easily into the frozen flesh.

When the wolf is finished, it nuzzles the salmon toward the girl, and the girl tears at the pink meat, discards the bones, swallows chunks whole.

I can't go back, the girl thinks as the salty pieces touch her tongue.

The wolf looks at her, and she imagines what it might say, what others (neighbor, preacher, uncle) have said before—it's not that bad, he's not that bad, it could be worse, at least he does this, at least he doesn't do that. And so she prepares herself, quiets that part of her, that restless part of her, the part that knows better, but this is a wolf sitting in front of the girl and not a neighbor, preacher, uncle, and maybe the wolf understands or maybe it doesn't, but it tilts its head and begins to howl, low and piercing through the icy night, and that restless part of the girl hears it, is shaken by it, awakened by it, and the restlessness moves its way up through her diaphragm and up, past her throat, her tongue, her teeth, and out into the night air, a cloud of growling moaning howl that, on such a clear winter night, reaches all the way for the moon.

HUMMINGBIRDS IN THE FOREST OF NEEDLE AND BLOOD

Ahimsa Timoteo Bodhrán

Say there is a boy in a village. Say the boy is not always a boy, but today he is. Say he is wandering by cactus, not wanting to be stuck by thorns, but wanting to smell the flowers and gather the fruits, not on each leaf, because he is not greedy, but rather enough to feed himself and his people. Say the boy is stuck by thorns and begins bleeding, gets worried, gets lost, gets stuck by more thorns. Say the boy collapses, exhausted, and he is not sure where his tears end and the blood begins. Say he is crying, and the sound echoes through the forest of nopal. Say the wind carries that sound to another boy, a boy whittling wood, sharpening stones. Say that boy drops what he is doing, and picks them up again, ties them with leather, and goes searching for that voice. Say that boy hurries, and he is pricked by thorns. Say that boy begins bleeding, and crying, but keeps moving through the forest of thorned ovals and red fruit, each heart glistening with its own blood. Say the boy begins to echo the first voice with his own, weaving it, tying it with leather. Say each boy gets louder, but they are still separated by walls. Say each boy is frantic, crying, trying to reach the other. Say the walls are covered with blood. Say the walls get thinner, thornier, and one hand grasps another. And the cactus is just a sheath of breath, leather between two hearts, raon-raon-light, colibrí-quick. Say the boys slow down till they can find an opening in the wall, crack they can leverage, space they can push their bodies through. Say there will be more blood, more tears, more cactus between them. Say it will not matter. Say the second boy will bind the wounds of the first boy with leather, wood to splint his leg, stone to dig out any thorns. Say the first boy will feed the second some fruit, blot his blood with petals, dust his cheeks and chest with pollen. Say the second boy will bind their wrists with leather, not too tight, but enough to keep them from getting lost. Say the first boy will place their things in his basket. Say the second boy will grab a stick to keep them walking. Say they keep walking. Say they keep bleeding. Say they keep crying. Say they leave the forest of needle and blood. Say they return to this place, again and again, and gently touch each leaf. Say the wind keeps their story. The ground, their stories. Say their descendants keep returning, generation after generation, to gather fruit, make offering of pollen, point to the place of dried red-brown on green-pricked leaves, higher up on the branches each year, leave some leather, newly cut, some stones, newly polished. Say the blood we drink from each fruit is their own. Say this is our story. Ours.

CONTRIBUTORS

MATT BARRETT is a writer from Pennsylvania. He teaches creative writing at Gettysburg College and holds an MFA in fiction from UNC-Greensboro. His stories have appeared or are forthcoming in the *Sun Magazine*, the *Threepenny Review*, the *Baltimore Review*, *SmokeLong Quarterly*, *Fractured Lit*, *Wigleaf*, *Cutleaf*, and *Best Microfiction 2022* and *2023*, among others.

DEMISTY D. BELLINGER lives and teaches in Massachusetts. Her chapbook, *Rubbing Elbows*, is available from Finishing Line Press. Some of her recent work can be found in *Contrary Magazine*, *Okay Donkey*, and *Best Small Fictions 2019*. DeMisty is online at demistybellinger.com.

AHIMSA TIMOTEO BODHRÁN is a multimedia artist, activist/organizer, critic, and educator. A Tulsa Artist Fellow and National Endowment for the Arts Fellow, he is the author of *Archipiélagos*, *Antes y después del Bronx: Lenapehoking*, and *South Bronx Breathing Lessons*. Bodhrán is editor of the international queer Indigenous issue of *Yellow Medicine Review: A Journal of Indigenous Literature, Art, and Thought*, and co-editor of the Native dance/movement/performance issue of *Movement Research Performance Journal*.

JAMY BOND's stories and essays have appeared in *Wigleaf*, the *Sun Magazine*, *The Rumpus*, *Pithead Chapel*, *Cheap Pop*, *JMWW*, *Ghost Parachute*, and elsewhere. Her work was selected for *Best Microfiction 2023* and appeared in the *Wigleaf* Top 50 2022 Longlist. She is a founding editor of *SugarSugarSalt Magazine*. Find her at jamybond.com and on Twitter at @bond_jamy.

MELISSA BOWERS is a writer from the Midwest. She is the winner of the SmokeLong Grand Micro Contest and a past winner of the *Breakwater Review*'s fiction prize, the *F(r)iction* flash fiction competition, and *The Writer*'s inaugural personal essay contest. Her work has been selected for the *Wigleaf* Top 50 as well as *Best Small Fictions*, and has also appeared in the *Cincinnati Review*, the *Greensboro Review*, *New Ohio Review*, *River Teeth*, *The Forge*, and the *Boston Globe Magazine*, among others. Read more at www.melissabowers.com or on Twitter at @MelissaBowers_.

MELISSA LLANES BROWNLEE (she/her), a native Hawaiian writer, living in Japan, has work published or forthcoming in *The Rumpus*, *Fractured Lit*, *Flash Frog*, *Gigantic Sequins*, *Cream City Review*, *Indiana Review*, and *Craft*. She is in *Best Small Fictions*, *Best Microfiction*, and the *Wigleaf* Top 50. Read *Hard Skin* (Juventud Press) and *Kahi and Lua* (Alien Buddha). She tweets at @lumchanmfa and talks story at www.melissallanesbrownlee.com.

MATT CANTOR is a surrealist from Boston, Massachusetts. He has been lucky to work with extraordinary filmmakers, musicians, and artists, and he'd be nowhere at all, of course, without his partner and his dog. It all comes from them, and he hopes someday it comes back to them. He was the winner of the 2021 Shelley A. Marshall Fiction Prize, and his work has been featured in *Fleas on the Dog*, *Teleport Magazine*, *The Other Folk*, *Once Upon a Crocodile*, *Funemployment*, and *Thieving Magpie*.

CHLOE N. CLARK is the author of *Patterns of Orbit*, *Collective Gravities*, and more. She is co-editor-in-chief of *Cotton Xenomorph*.

LILLY DANCYGER is the author of *First Love* (Dial Press, 2024), a collection of personal and critical essays about the power and complexity of female friendship; and *Negative Space* (SFWP, 2021), a reported and illustrated memoir selected by Carmen Maria Machado as a winner of the Santa Fe Writers Project Literary Awards. Find her on Twitter at @lillydancyger.

CAROLINE MACON FLEISCHER lives in Chicago with her husband, son, and pets. She is the author of the psychological thriller *The Roommate* (2022) and the horror novel *A Play About a Curse* (forthcoming 2024). More of her writing has been published in *Oh Reader*, LitHub's *CrimeReads*, *American Theatre Magazine*, and others. She is the cofounder and editor of the small chapbook publisher Fruit Bat Press and teaches creative writing at Loyola University and the Theatre School at DePaul.

KELSEY FRANCIS's work has appeared in *Porcupine Literary*, *HAD*, *Twin Pies Literary*, the *Washington Post*, *Adirondack Life Magazine*, and the "Modern Love" column of the *New York Times*, among others. She lives, teaches, and writes in the Adirondack Mountains of Upstate New York. She can be found on Twitter at @ADK_Kelsey.

LORI YEGHIAYAN FRIEDMAN's most recent work has appeared in *Longleaf Review*, *Pangyrus*, *Pithead Chapel*, *Memoir Monthly*, and the *Los Angeles Times*. Her creative nonfiction has twice been nominated for a Pushcart Prize. She has an MFA in theater from UC San Diego and attended the Tin House Winter Workshop 2023. Follow her on Twitter: @loriyeg.

CAROLJEAN GAVIN's work has appeared in places such as *Milk Candy Review*, *Fractured*, *New World Writing*, *Best Small Fictions*, and *X-R-A-Y Literary Magazine*. She's the author of *Shards of a Stained-Glass Moving Picture Fairytale* (Selcouth Station Press). She's on Twitter at @caroljeangavin.

KATE GEHAN's debut short story collection, *The Girl and the Fox Pirate*, was published by Mojave River Press in 2018. Her writing has appeared in *SmokeLong Quarterly*, *McSweeney's Internet Tendency*, *Split Lip Magazine*, *People Holding*, and *Cheap Pop*, among others. Find her work at kategehan.com.

MIRIAM GERSHOW is the author of *The Local News* and the forthcoming *Survival Tips: Stories* and *Closer*. Her flash fiction appears in a variety of places, including *Pithead Chapel*, *Heavy Feather Review*, and *Variant Lit*, where "Lines of Communication" won the first annual Variant Literature Pizza Prize.

ANNA GATES HA is a writer from Northern California. Her short fiction, nominated twice for the Pushcart Prize, has appeared in *Longleaf Review*, *Fractured Lit*, *Citron Review*, and others. She received her MFA from Saint Mary's College of California.

KATHLEEN MCKITTY HARRIS is a fifth-generation native New Yorker whose work has been published in the *New York Times*, *Longreads*, *Creative Nonfiction*, *McSweeney's*, and *The Rumpus*, among others. Kathleen also performs as a storyteller, and has been featured on *The Moth Podcast* and on such stages as Joe's Pub at the Public Theater in New York City. She cohosts the "What's Your Story?" reading series in northern New Jersey, where she lives with her husband and two children. Follow her on social media: @kmckharris.

MATTHEW E. HENRY (MEH) is the author of *the Colored Page* (Sundress Publications, 2022), *Teaching While Black* (Main Street Rag, 2020), and *Dust & Ashes* (Californios Press, 2020). He has three collections forthcoming in 2023 *The Third Renunciation* (New York Quarterly Books), *Have You Heard the One About…?* (Ghost City Press), and *Said the Frog to the Scorpion* (Harbor Editions). He is editor-in-chief of the *Weight Journal* and an associate poetry editor at *Pidgeonholes*.

AUBREY HIRSCH is the author of a short story collection, *Why We Never Talk About Sugar* and a 2022 National Endowment for the Arts Fellow in Literature. Her stories, essays, and comics have appeared in *Time*, the *New York Times*, the *Washington Post*, *Black Warrior Review*, *American Short Fiction*, and elsewhere. You can learn more about her at http://aubreyhirsch.com.

EMILY JAMES is a teacher and writer in New York City. She is the managing editor at *Pidgeonholes* and a founding editor of *Porcupine Literary*. She's the winner of the 2020 Baltimore Review CNF Contest, a SmokeLong Flash 2020 finalist, and the winner of the 2019 Bechtel Prize. Her work can be found in *Guernica*, *River Teeth*, the *Atticus Review*, *Jellyfish Review*, and elsewhere.

RUTH JOFFRE is the author of the story collection *Night Beast*. Her work has appeared or is forthcoming in more than fifty publications, including *Lightspeed*, *Pleiades*, *khré*, the *Florida Review Online*, *Reckoning*, and the anthologies *Best Microfiction 2021* and *2022*. She served as the 2020–2022 Prose Writer-in-Residence at Hugo House and as a Visiting Writer at University of Washington Bothell in 2023.

DAVON LOEB is the author of the memoir *The In-Betweens*. He earned an MFA in creative writing from Rutgers University-Camden. Davon is an assistant features editor at *The Rumpus*. His work is featured in the *Sun Magazine*, the *Los Angeles Times*, *Joyland Magazine*, *Gulf Coast Journal*, *Catapult*, *Ploughshares*, and elsewhere.

DW MCKINNEY is a writer and editor based in Nevada. A 2023 Periplus Fellow, her work has appeared in *Los Angeles Review of Books*, *Ecotone*, the *Normal School*, *TriQuarterly*, and *Hippocampus Magazine*, among others. Her nonfiction was a finalist for *december* magazine's 2022 Curt Johnson Prose Award and *Hippocampus Magazine*'s 2020 Remember in November Contest for Creative Nonfiction. She is also a nonfiction editor for *Shenandoah*. Send some love to dwmckinney.com.

K.C. MEAD-BREWER is an author living in beautiful Baltimore, Maryland. She writes mostly weird, dark fiction, the kind of stories that love flashlights, closets, and the green dark between the trees. For more, check out her website: kcmeadbrewer.com.

EDIE MEADE is a writer, artist, and musician in Petersburg, Virginia. Recent work can be found in *Invisible City*, *New Flash Fiction Review*, *Atlas & Alice*, the *Normal School*, *Pidgeonholes*, and elsewhere.

SARAH FAWN MONTGOMERY is the author of *Halfway from Home* (Split/Lip Press, 2022), *Quite Mad: An American Pharma Memoir* (Ohio State University Press, 2018), and three poetry chapbooks. She is an associate professor at Bridgewater State University.

ELLEN BIRKETT MORRIS is the author of *Lost Girls*, winner of the Pencraft Award and finalist for the Clara Johnson, Independent Author Network, and Best Book awards. Her novel *Beware the Tall Grass* won the Donald L. Jordan Award for Literary Excellence (CSU Press, March 2024). Her fiction has appeared in *Shenandoah* and *Antioch Review*, among other journals. She won the Bevel Summers Prize for short fiction. Morris has a fellowship for her fiction from the Kentucky Arts Council.

HEMA NATARAJU is an Indian American writer, mom, and polyglot currently based in Singapore. Her work has most recently appeared in *Barrelhouse, Bending Genres, Five South, Booth, Wigleaf, 100 Word Story*, and *Ruby Literary*, among others. She is a submissions editor at *SmokeLong Quarterly* and tweets as @m_ixedbag.

MEGHA NAYAR is a language coach and fiction writer from/in India. She teaches English and French for a living, and writes short stories to claim her place in the world. Her work has appeared in over forty literary magazines. She is currently working on her maiden collection of short stories. Twitter: @meghasnatter.

DEESHA PHILYAW's debut short story collection, *The Secret Lives of Church Ladies*, won the 2021 PEN/Faulkner Award for Fiction, the 2020/21 Story Prize, and the 2020 LA Times Book Prize: Art Seidenbaum Award for First Fiction, and was a finalist for the 2020 National Book Award for Fiction. *The Secret Lives of Church Ladies* focuses on Black women, sex, and the Black church, and is being adapted for television by HBO Max with Tessa Thompson executive producing. Deesha is also a Kimbilio Fiction Fellow and was the 2022–2023 John and Renée Grisham Writer-in-Residence at the University of Mississippi.

ZACH POWERS is the author of the novel *First Cosmic Velocity* (Putnam, 2019) and the story collection *Gravity Changes* (BOA Editions, 2017). His writing has been featured by *American Short Fiction, Lit Hub*, the *Washington Post*, and elsewhere. He serves as artistic director for the Writer's Center and

Poet Lore, America's oldest poetry magazine. Originally from Savannah, Georgia, he now lives in Arlington, Virginia. Get to know him at ZachPowers.com.

AURELEO SANS is a Colombian American, nonbinary, queer, formerly unhoused writer and poet with a disability who resides in San Antonio, Texas. She has been named a Sewanee Writers' Conference Scholar, a Tin House Scholar, a Roots Wounds Words Writers Retreat Fellow, a Lambda Literary Fellow, an ASF Workshop Fellow, and a Periplus Fellow. Her work has appeared in *Shenandoah*, *Salamander*, *Electric Literature*, *Passages North*, the *2023 Best Micro Fiction Anthology*, and elsewhere.

ALYSIA LI YING SAWCHYN is editor-in-chief of *The Rumpus*. Her debut essay collection, *A Fish Growing Lungs* (2020), was a finalist for the Believer Awards in nonfiction. She has received fellowships from the Sewanee Writers' Conference and the Kenyon Writers' Workshop, and teaches nonfiction at Warren Wilson College.

The daughter of Chinese immigrants, **JEN SOONG** grew up in New Jersey and received her MFA in creative writing from UC Davis. An alum of Tin House and VONA, her writing has appeared in the *Washington Post*, the *Audacity*, and *Waxwing*. Her memoir-in-progress is a reckoning with myth and memory.

AMBER SPARKS is the author of an upcoming novel, *Happy People Don't Live Here*, and four collections of short fiction, including *And I Do Not Forgive You: Revenges and Other Stories* and *The Unfinished World*; and her fiction and essays have appeared in *American Short Fiction*, the *Paris Review*, *Slate*, *Tin House*, *Granta*, *The Cut*, and elsewhere. She lives in Washington, DC, with her husband, daughter, and two cats.

AMY STUBER's work has appeared in *Flash Fiction America*, *Missouri Review*, *New England Review*, and elsewhere. She serves as flash fiction editor at *Split Lip Magazine*.

MICHAEL B. TAGER is a writer and the managing editor of Mason Jar Press. His work has been published, is very good, and can be found at Michaelbtager.com. He's the author of *The Pop Culture Poetry Collection: Definitive Edition* (Akinoga Press, 2024). He's most creative in the morning, most productive at night, and kind of worthless in the midafternoon.

SARAH TOLLOK, a multigenre writer, lives in the beautiful Shenandoah Valley of Virginia. Sarah has a story in the anthology *Things Improbable* with Improbable Press, and will be included in an upcoming anthology with Clandestine Press. Her debut book, *Bookstories*, will be published by Balance of Seven in 2024. You can find Sarah on Twitter and Goodreads by name, on Instagram as Sarah_Tollok_author_reader, and at SarahTollok.com.

HANANAH ZAHEER is the author of *Lovebirds* (Bull City Press, 2021). Recent work has appeared in *Pleiades*, *Kenyon Review*, *Best Small Fictions 2021*, and elsewhere. She won the Lawrence Foundation prize for fiction, and her story "Fish Tank" was a notable mention in *Best American Short Stories*. She is the founder of Dubai Literary Salon (a prose reading series), a fiction editor for *SAAG*, and a fiction editor for the *Los Angeles Review*.

TARA ISABEL ZAMBRANO is a writer of color and is the author of a full-length flash collection, *Death, Desire, And Other Destinations* by Okay Donkey Press. She is an electrical engineer by profession and lives in Texas.

ACKNOWLEDGMENTS

Thanks are due to the following publications in which these stories originally appeared, some in different form:

"A Girl Attends a Pep Rally," by Ruth Joffre, first appeared in *The Forge*.

"More Fun in the New World," by Amy Stuber, first appeared in *Ninth Letter*.

"How to Reverse Time When You're Tired of Being the Hero," by Amber Sparks, first appeared in *Barrelhouse*.

"Hive Mind," by Melissa Bowers, first appeared in *The Forge*.

"Surface Treatments," by Zach Powers, first appeared in *American Short Fiction*.

"Solve for Ways to Disappear," by Alysia Sawchyn, first appeared in *Burrow Press Review*.

"Lines of Communication," by Miriam Gershow, first appeared in *Variant Lit*.

"Inheritance," by Ellen Birkett Morris, first appeared in *Lost Girls: Short Stories*.

"Feeding Time," by Jen Soong, first appeared in *Witness*.

"Pocketed," by Sarah Fawn Montgomery, first appeared in *Lost Balloon*.

"Hummingbirds in the Forest of Needle and Blood," by Ahimsa Timoteo Bodhrán, first appeared in *1110*.